Landscape Ideas You Can Use

How to Choose **Structures, Surfaces** & **Plants**
That Transform Your Yard

CHRIS PETERSON

**Creative Publishing
international**

MINNEAPOLIS, MINNESOTA
www.creativepub.com

**Creative Publishing
international**

Copyright © 2012
Creative Publishing international, Inc.
400 First Avenue North, Suite 300
Minneapolis, Minnesota 55401
1-800-328-0590
www.creativepub.com

Printed in China

10 9 8 7 6 5 4 3 2 1

Library of Congress Cataloging-in-Publication Data

Peterson, Chris,
Landscape Ideas you can use / Chris Peterson.
  p. cm.
  ISBN-13: 978-1-58923-701-8 (pbk.)
  ISBN-10: 1-58923-701-3 (soft cover)
  1. Decks (Architecture, Domestic) I. Title.
  TH4970.P474 2011
  690'.184--dc22
                         2011009688

President/CEO: Ken Fund
Group Publisher: Bryan Trandem

Home Improvement Group

Associate Publisher: Mark Johanson
Developmental Editor: Jordan Wiklund
Creative Director: Michele Lanci
Design Manager: Brenda C. Canales
Production Managers: Laura Hokkanen, Linda Halls

Author: Chris Peterson
Page Layout Artist: Helena Shimizu
Copy Editor: Ingrid Sundstrom Lundegaard

Contents

Introduction

The difference between a landscape and a yard is thoughtful design. A yard is simply the space outside your front or back door. You might slap a deck or patio down, park a grill off to one side, or throw some shade-loving annuals over in the dark corner if you have time on a spring weekend. A landscape, on the other hand, is developed element by element. It is a space as well-designed as any room in the house.

As such, landscaping is purposefully created according to a theme and follows certain principles. The theme can be wild or formal, subtle or bold. The principles center around five basic elements that form any landscape design: line, form, mass, texture, and color. The first three are the backbone. The last two are the skin and clothes that add visual richness and depth. Like everything else in a landscape design, lines should be intentional; curving lines are less formal, and guide the eye, providing a sense of motion and action. Straight lines and angles are a more formal approach. They are a great way to succinctly organize the landscape or replicate lines in the home's architecture or natural lines in the topography.

A mix of plant shapes, heights, and forms adds visual interest to any landscape. Most often, you'll use natural shapes to complement or contrast one another. You can, however, use repetitive plantings to create a pleasing rhythm within the landscape. Texture and color should be threads you run through the design, deliberately placed to complement or contrast other colors or textures.

That all may sound a bit fancy and academic, but it's not. It boils down to this—you build a successful landscape one piece at a time. Your theme guides your decisions, including path style, plants, surfaces, and all the other choices you make for the landscape. Theme even determines the best accents to finish your design—from water features to statuary, structures such as arbors and gates, and ornaments such as gazing balls or sundials.

Still don't know where to start? You've come to the right place. The pages of this book are organized to cover just about every element and landscape design situation you might encounter. You'll find a variety of compelling images to inspire and ignite your imagination and innovative ideas that you might want to consider for your own backyard (or front yard) oasis. It doesn't matter if your outdoor space is small or large, sloped or flat, woodsy or suburban— there are tons of possibilities in the sections that follow. Put them to good use to move beyond the "yard," and into the landscape of your dreams.

BE UP FRONT. It's easy to forget the front yard when planning your landscape, but that's a mistake. The varied beds bracketing the front door of this house feature a profusion of flowers and shrubs. The planting is composed so that the mass increases closer to the house. This guides the eye up from the lawn, to the structure of the house, and provides a lovely, soft visual transition from the flat to the vertical.

ADD NIGHT-LIGHTS. The landscape at night can be every bit as much a draw as it is during the day. Proper lighting is key, both for safety and to illuminate the charm of your design. The pool in this yard is incredibly alluring lit from within, while the fire pit is a fascinating focal point that fairly screams, "Sit and relax." Notice the open-grid design of the outdoor floor—it's a great treatment to blur the distinction between plant life and hardscape.

MAKE YOUR FENCES FANCY. Fences can be far more than simple privacy barriers. You can use fencing to partition off interior areas, as a way to create small, intimate areas within the larger landscape plan. You can also use fencing as it is in this yard, as a design element in and of itself. The simple, repetitive vertical lines of this fence create a continuity that ties together different areas in a rambling landscape. Think carefully about the style of any fence you build—it may be the perfect opportunity to accent your landscape.

Introduction

DIVIDE YOUR SPACE. Creating separate outdoor "rooms" is a wonderful technique for designing around a large open expanse, such as a lawn. Here, a hedge and trellis arbor offer a visual boundary that creates a sense of mystery of what lies on the other side. The best landscape designs draw a visitor through the landscape and that's exactly what's happening here. The homeowner has used the open area of the lawn to frame an interesting focal point—a wheelbarrow planter.

DOUBLE-DOWN ON ROMANCE. This is the traditional tiered "pineapple" fountain that suits many different styles of landscape or garden. The wide basin makes this a good choice for a bird garden because it doubles as a birdbath. The look is not ideal for informal gardens such as a country or cottage style, but it fits right in almost everywhere else. One of the great things about fountains like these is that you can use them as hidden-away surprise visuals, or as focal points in their own right, placed in the middle of a lawn, garden bed, or courtyard.

USE ODD NUMBERS. Water features are some of the most fascinating landscape elements. The koi pond in this large, wild landscape is accented with ceramic urns equipped with pumps so that they serve as fountains. It's an informal, stylish look that is perfectly suited to the naturalistic surroundings. The use of three urns is intentional: the eye finds odd numbers of objects more interesting and intriguing than even numbers.

MIX MATERIALS TO BUILD VISUAL INTEREST. Effective, livable landscaping often entails creating different areas—different outdoor rooms—for different purposes. One side of this large yard has been dedicated to a sitting area defined by an open-spaced, square-cut stone patio with pebble infill. Bordered by groundcover and ornamental grasses, this area is as close to zero maintenance as you can get, and is also a drought-tolerant design.

Introduction

DIRECT TRAFFIC. Use arbors, pergolas, archways, or gates as invitations, leading people where you want them to go in the landscape. Wood is an obvious choice for these types of structures because the material blends in well with the plant life in a lush landscape. A simple vine has been trained on this pergola with trellis side panels, softening the lines of the structure and further melding it into the surrounding landscape.

TRY TERRACING. Slopes can be a big challenge for the home landscaper. There are lots of ways to deal with a slope, but one of the best and longest lasting techniques is to terrace the slope. This front yard features stacked timber retaining walls to create terraces filled with evergreens. It's a well-defined, easy solution that could successfully be applied to many different sloped sites. The solution is also fairly inexpensive—never a bad thing in a landscape design.

FREEFORM IS FUN. There are an amazing variety of pathway styles to choose from for your landscape. The stepping stones used in this setting are a simple-to-install option that can be arranged to accommodate just about any layout, such as following the shape of the lawn here. Stepping stones are excellent when used in or across an expanse of lawn, because mowing over them is a cinch. The look is informal, though, and you should be sure that it matches the design style you're trying to set.

MAKE ROOM FOR ART. Landscape sculpture can be the perfect way to put your fingerprints on a design. Sculpture should be carefully chosen not only to suit the style of your landscape, but also to ensure that it survives the elements and ages well. A single sculpture is often more effective than a group or scattered collection throughout a garden or landscape. The abstract metal piece here perfectly complements the informal bed of trees and ornamental grasses in which it's placed. It will fit in just as well as it ages and acquires a lovely patina of rust.

CREATE AN OUTDOOR FLOOR. Hardscaping—the use of hard surfaces in landscaping—offers great potential to get creative. Not only can you choose from a wealth of paving styles and materials, you can mix and match for dynamic effect. This mortar-set includes a formal linear field of bricks in various sizes and shapes, a thin border of flat black sliced pebbles, and an outer border of small, irregular stone pieces. It's enough to steal attention from any garden scene.

Before

After

TAKE WHAT YOUR LANDSCAPE WILL GIVE. The lawn fronting this southern home suffered mightily under the hot-weather climate, and was a drain on limited water resources. Replacing the surface with a xeriscaped design full of low-maintenance and drought-tolerant grasses and perennials makes more practical sense and is a fantastic upgrade to the look of the yard. Always keep in mind that a clever landscape design can solve problems as well as add beauty and order to the yard.

Landscaping Styles

Some yards are blank canvasses waiting to be painted. Your house may be a basic structure that doesn't urge you in any particular design direction, and the local plant life and terrain may not be particularly distinctive. In this case, the door is wide open for you to choose a landscape style that reflects your tastes, suits the layout of your yard, and nurtures the way you want to live in your outdoor room.

In other cases, the local environment and surroundings may provide very strong indicators of an appropriate landscape style. You'd be wise to listen to these cues. For instance, if your home is located in a desert region of a southwestern state, you'll probably want to develop your landscape design around certain plants and features common to the area, including succulents, water-conserving hardscape and groundcovers, and shade structures. A cottage garden would simply not fit and would always look like a sore thumb—just as a desert landscape would look wrong attached to a New England home.

The location of your home may allow for multiple design possibilities. A coastal home that isn't on the water, for example, could look great with a sand-strewn seaside landscape, a Mediterranean villa look, a cottage garden style, or even a formal design.

ECHO YOUR ENVIRONMENT. It is often best if the landscape style takes its cues from the surrounding geography and climate. This is especially true when the environment and terrain are distinctive as with a seaside home, or the high chaparral shown here. The design of this large yard takes advantage of the bordering wide-open plain and mountain views by leaving the property undefined by a fence or row of trees. The native terrain is allowed to blend into the yard, and along with terraced patios, native plants are used sparsely, in keeping with the practical realities of the drought-prone region. An antique horse-drawn wagon is used as yard sculpture to reinforce the open-plains feel of the yard.

Start by looking at plants and outdoor structures in your area. Look beyond other yards to parks and botanical gardens that often present many different styles of landscaping. When you've narrowed in on a sense of the style that most appeals to you and would be most appropriate for your home and yard, begin refining your ideas by checking out the images on the following pages.

REPEAT. REPEAT. The trim, straight lines and spare aesthetic of a modern home begs for the same treatment in its landscape. The designer of this front yard has obliged, using simple, repetitive plantings featuring regimented rows of spiky foliage plants with plenty of space left between the plants. The beds are formed of the same geometric shapes that dominate the walkway and the house itself. The modern look has a bonus feature of a water-conserving, low maintenance landscape.

LESS MAY BE MORE. Modern architecture is all about linear perspective and minimal ornamentation. Marrying a landscape to a modern house can be challenging, but not if you throw out the conventional wisdom of what a landscape should be. Here, a curving bed provides a modicum of visual relief from the hard lines that define both yard and house. The bed is planted with drought-tolerant, hot-weather species that require little in the way of upkeep. A lawn of hot-climate grass will go brown when dormant in the hottest part of the summer, but cut short it will still have a clean, sharp look in keeping with the rest of the design. When it comes to modern-style landscapes, less is often more.

Wooded Retreat

SHOW OFF YOUR SHADE. Hardscaping such as the patio and garden wall shown here is the ideal way to define social and recreational areas within a wooded yard. The trees are left standing and undisturbed, and the use of natural stone fits right into the surroundings. Shade-loving annuals are excellent choices to bring seasonal color into the dappled landscape.

KEEP IT NATURAL. Landscaping a wooded yard sometimes means bending to the will of the environment. This yard features shade-loving grass in a lawn without edging and native wildflower and shrub plantings that would normally be found in a regional forest. The trick in working with a wooded landscape design is to balance the wholly natural appeal of a dense copse of trees, with the variation the eye expects in a designed landscape.

CREATE "SUNSHINE" ON A SHADY DAY. Any landscape bordering a wooded area must account for the potentially deep shade under leafed-out trees. This bed of shade-loving plants fills the bill perfectly, providing lush full shapes and many shades of green. A few flowering plants add splashes of color and a rambling stone border goes perfectly with the rustic setting.

WEATHERED CAN BE WONDERFUL. Complement a woodsy landscape setting with appropriately rustic structures. The weathered split-log swing in this yard has a timeworn look that fits right in with the overgrown, landscape. Gray planter boxes add perfect accents to the structure and hold splashes of color in the form of seasonal flowers. Match landscape structures to your design style for a unified theme that holds together perfectly.

The Formal Garden

COMBINE CLASSIC PATTERNS. Distinctive architecture often sets a tone that the landscape can follow. Stone walls offer a stately look that is complemented by an entryway and side yard paved with a sophisticated brick pattern. A simple fence with latticework top panel and carriage lights provides a fitting boundary, while beds lined with trimmed ball-shaped shrubs and a three-tier fountain add a dignified polish to this design.

PRUNE A SHRUB OR TREE TO ADD FORMALITY. Formal landscapes are defined by particular elements. Repetitive features such as the planters in this yard—and cultivated shapes like the topiary that occupy those planters—are both strong indicators of formal landscape style. Straight lines are another, established here in the weathered decking. If you're after a formal aesthetic, consider features such as these to define the look.

GET FORMAL IN FRONT. A formal garden does not need to be the size of a royal estate to be appealing. It can even be located in the front of the house—it helps if the architectural style of the house is on the formal side, like the Georgian home seen here. One archetypal form found in formal gardens is rectangularity, here created by the neatly clipped boxwood hedgerow and the straight rows of terra cotta edging. Certain elements also lend formality, including Grecian-style urns, pedestals and fountains or a well-sited, classic park bench.

Magical Cottage Gardens

YOU CAN'T GO WRONG WITH ROSES. Cottage gardens are all about tumbles of flowering plants cascading across the landscape—especially roses. It's a joyously untidy, unconstrained look that seems haphazard and overgrown. In reality, cottage gardens require a good amount of maintenance to keep all the blooming plants healthy. You may fall in love with the romantic look, but unless you have a green thumb, think twice about trying to replicate this style in your own yard.

TRAIN YOUR PLANTS WELL. A cottage-garden landscape style is best suited to small yards, and buildings that reinforce the style, such as Victorians, stone buildings, and of course, cottages. Training climbing plants—both roses and blooming vines—is a key part of the look. Lawn surfaces should be kept to a minimum and bordered by sprawling plants and blooming shrubs.

ACCESSORIES ADD WHIMSY. Gazing balls are wonderful touches appropriate for both formal and cottage gardens (they date from the Victorian period, one of the golden ages of flower gardening). A birdbath is also a great idea in this type of landscaping style; the profusion of blooming plants will naturally draw birds, as well as bees and butterflies. Notice the casual, almost happenstance look of the pathway. Every detail in a cottage garden should look a little timeworn to make the style appeal authentic, but still designed with an eye toward sound basics of line, massing, and colors.

A LITTLE GINGERBREAD GOES A LONG WAY. Few accents scream cottage garden like a white picket fence. Add a trellis gate covered with scented climbing roses and the scene is just about complete. Recognizable elements like this fence are good places to start with your landscape design, because they help establish a definitive style and give you blocks on which you can build. A picket fence is fairly easy to build from sections readily available at large home centers and some nurseries. Make your life easier by buying prefab panels and materials as much as possible—it will allow you to focus more effort on your plantings.

THINK THEATRICALLY. A big expanse of lawn is like a stage on which you can compose elements. Beds, trees, and other features can be unified into a coherent landscape design by wrapping lawn around them or vice versa. It's the thread that holds the look together. A peninsula patio such as the one in this yard becomes a platform for the audience—a place to not only unwind, but to enjoy the interplay of elements amid a sea of green.

CURVED BORDERS SOFTEN LINES. The front yard lawn is a traditional landscaping element for the American home. But there's simply no need or excuse to settle for a boring green rectangle unaccompanied by any other signs of life. As this image clearly demonstrates, a variety of plantings creates a unique interplay between the solid green, flat surface and a mixture of plant colors and shapes. This front yard incorporates small trees, a trio of tall arbor vitae standing like guardians before the house, and a beautiful shrub bed with a scattering of mixed colors. Trees in containers add even more of an interest to the lawn's smooth, unvarying surface.

SMALL LAWNS HAVE BIG IMPACT. The curving inside border of this attractive small lawn lets the entryway plantings garner attention. A thin concrete edging provides a crisp, clean look to both lawn and borders and serves as a mowing strip. Mowing strips are great ideas wherever a lawn meets a bed or border—they make mowing the lawn less of an adventure and create a tidy appearance because the grass line is contained and mulch material is less likely to scatter over the lawn.

CREATE A RIVER OF GRASS. Lawns can be a great solution for long, slightly graded slopes such as this. Beds on either side of this "bowling green" provide plenty of interest. Evergreens, flowering bulbs, and other plants fill the view, and the trim lawn looks elegant between the massed borders. Notice that a path has been laid alongside the lawn to limit wear and tear on the grass itself. Too much traffic on any lawn in your landscape can lead to compaction and unsightly brown or worn spots.

Suburban Subtle

SHAKE UP YOUR SYMMETRY. Suburban landscapes are often marked by symmetry, such as the two trees on either side of this home and the matching foundation plantings that mark the front border of the porch. But it's always good to include at least one asymmetrical element to keep the look lively. Here, a low-lying shrub bed curves out on one side of the front walkway, which itself curves off to the side, adding visual interest. Always keep in mind that it's okay to use squares and rectangles in your landscape, but if they're the only shapes, things can start to look boring.

A HEALTHY LAWN MAKES A POSITIVE STATEMENT. Most suburban landscapes tend to be low-maintenance—precisely the point of the large yard that graces this two-story house. Mature trees overlook a regimented border of shrubs that need trimming no more than once a year. The large expanse of lawn requires mowing once a week, but in-ground sprinklers on an automatic system keep the lawn from getting thirsty and brown. In-ground sprinklers with computer controlled watering are a great choice for any large lawn surface in a landscape. The homeowner here has gone the extra distance to create lawn-mowing stripes, a classic look.

INVEST IN A FEW GOOD TREES. A tree can be a wonderful way to break up the staid suburban formula of lawn coupled with foundation plantings. This specimen was the perfect selection, maturing to a graceful shape that is in ideal proportion to the house. Always research the type of tree you're buying to ensure that it will look good in the landscape over time. Faster growing species are available, but in most cases you should plan on 15 to 20 years before a tree is mature.

VENTURE OFF THE BEATEN PATH. A way to break out of the confines of homeowner association rules and the oversight of neighbors is to include an unusual element in your landscape. Pick one that isn't so far out that it draws glares, but is distinctive enough to set your home apart. Irregularly spaced stepping stones sunk into the grass is an innovative front walk for this house—unique but not strange, and a providing great visual impact for such a small feature.

SEEK TRANQUILITY. Designers of Japanese gardens create drama from natural forms in the landscape. Typical of the style, slab steps seem to float up out of the earth in this garden, and a small evergreen has been manicured into tree form with cloud-shaped greenery. The idea behind each element is subtlety and restraint and a truly organic feel, as if nature itself had decided to lay a path or trim a tree.

GET CENTERED. Decorative sculptures are often a part of Japanese-style landscapes. The design rarely incorporates more than one, and the sculpture is usually a culturally significant representation. This mini pagoda sculpture is typical, although seated Buddha sculptures are frequently used as well. The sculpture is usually nested among dense plantings and less often used as a centerpiece for a raked stone or sand bed.

CREATE FLOW. This design includes a lawn of moisture-sipping hot weather grasses and a recirculating water feature of three bowls that cascade one into the other and fill a small meditation pond. The elements are simple and basic, but the composition—from the flat lawn, medium height fountain, and the façade of the home and tall palms in the background—is just perfect. Palm trees are a natural addition in thirsty landscapes, and a wonderful shape to add to any hot-climate yard.

RAKE YOUR CARES AWAY. Perhaps the most decorative use for boulders is as sculptural features inside the field of a stone bed in a Zen garden design. This distinctive look really only works in that particular style, but it is stunning. The boulders are specifically chosen to look as if they have burst forth from the earth and are growing out of the bed of raked stone. It's an almost poetic look that is unforgettable when executed correctly.

CHOOSE RUSTIC FURNISHINGS. A pole arbor and matching bench provide a restful retreat in the middle of a foliage-dense country-style setting. Structures like arbors, trellises, planters, and fences are great ways to announce a style amid plantings that could cross over between several different looks. This structure with its overhead vine exclaims "country" through and through.

CAPTURE CHAOS. Detailed screens, a pergola, and extensive decking bring order to this landscape, but the plantings themselves are all about abundant chaos. They spring from containers, sprawl through spaces in the screens and tumble over borders everywhere. This is a great way to use contrast to your advantage—attractive, ornate, and orderly structures offset by unruly, spectacular plantings to provide stunning surroundings.

TAKE A WALK ON THE WILD SIDE. Lush as far as the eye can see, this wild garden features a fieldstone pathway through a dense cascade of plants. The plants are grouped so tightly that they appear as one seamless mass—a key feature of wild plantings. The mix includes low-lying and tall shrubs, sprawling ground covers such as creeping thyme, and flowers woven through ferns and other shade-loving foliage plants. Wild gardens are all about a mix of plants jostling one another for supremacy.

INVITE THE GARDENS IN FOR A VISIT. A front porch is the perfect spot for a wild country garden. Add one wood bench with distressed paint, mix in a variety of vines grown haphazardly around the structure of the porch, combine with a few planters that look like odds and ends, place it all in a yard filled with green sprawling plants, and you have the characteristics of a wild garden: untamed look, healthy unruly plants, and structures that look natural.

Landscaping by Yard Size

Yard size affects landscape design in several ways. The features that will be appropriate for the landscape are often dependent on the size you have available. A large tree or significant water feature such as a reflecting pool may simply overwhelm a smaller yard. The styles you can choose will also be affected by yard size. For instance, a formal design can look uncomfortable constrained in a tiny space, but a cottage garden is right at home in a small yard.

Start with the number and complexity of features and plantings. A small yard looks best when it incorporates one or two focal features, supported with plantings and surrounding background elements. Look for space-appropriate versions of popular structures and fixtures. Instead of a large centerpiece fountain, a wall fountain may be more in keeping with your yard size.

Medium-sized yards increase the possibilities. Some are given over to swimming pools, with the surrounding landscape design and plantings serving to make the pool look as natural as possible. A medium-sized yard also allows you more flexibility in creating landscape mystery—a pathway winding out of sight into some concealed "secret garden" or restful refuge where you can hide away for a few contemplative moments.

CELEBRATE DIVERSITY. Just because a yard is small doesn't mean it can't be diverse. And just because it's a front yard doesn't mean it has to follow some stereotypical formula for a lawn, spread out in front of foundation plantings. The designer of this front yard added a wedge-shaped bed with containers and a variety of plants. The shape itself adds a lot of visual interest, while a stone wall in front of the house creates the perception of visual depth.

Large yards are brimming with design potential. Two realities will, however, limit what you can do: expense and the time you can dedicate to maintenance. Large landscapes are often designed with sweeping open vistas serving the same role as empty "negative" space does in painting—to give rhythm and pacing to the overall design. Whether these spaces are hardscaped or grass, they usually entail less maintenance than a full-blown garden. Large yards also present the chance to include several different and distinct areas, such as a rose garden, lawn for recreation, and a pond. Use a pathway to unify disparate areas.

No matter how big your yard is, never let the size make you give up on good landscape design. Use a little creativity and the ideas shown here to find a beautiful solution for your yard, no matter what size it is.

PACK IT IN. Small-yard landscaping is all about maximizing potential. This eclectic design fits a lot into a tiny space. The centerpiece is a decorative brick seating circle with a path featuring bricks laid in a different direction. The design includes two shaped shrubs, a lovely detailed gate and fence, perennials and shade-loving groundcovers, and even a tomato plant in the middle of the front bed. The design leaves no lack of visual interest no matter where you're looking.

BUILD UPWARD. Pergolas are wonderful structures for all yards, but they are an especially handy option if you're designing a small or medium-sized landscape. Pergola designs are usually scalable, so that they can be altered to suit available dimensions. They clearly define a central area in the landscape (usually used for relaxation, socializing or both). They not only shade that area, allowing pleasantly mottled sunlight to come through, they can also support all manner of climbing plants—allowing you to go vertical with your garden greenery where space is at a premium.

CREATE A HIGHLIGHT WITH A PLUG-AND-PLAY WATER FEATURE. Looking for a wonderful water feature for your tiny backyard? You could do a lot worse than an urn fountain. These are self-contained, easy to install, have a small footprint, and look great in landscape styles from contemporary to Japanese, to eclectic and beyond. Urns come in many sizes, and with glazes in different colors including deep blue, red, and earthy browns. An arrangement like the one shown here, with the urn placed on an artful bed of polished river rocks, is effective.

PICK A STAR PLAYER. A small yard, plus one stunning focal point, equals major design success. The designer here created a meditative spot out of a postage stamp of real estate, using simple, spare, and elegant elements. The neatly bordered grass is a foil for a one-of-a-kind vertical fountain and sculpture. Tightly pruned small trees reinforce a look of order and calm. The lesson is this: when dealing with your own small space, consider using one spectacular focal point along with supporting players that reinforce the style.

Before

After

APPLY INTERIOR DECORATING PRINCIPLES. A miniscule side yard with little direct sun can be a big challenge, as it was for this homeowner. Ivy had taken over, a sole shrub struggled to survive, and the fence and pavers looked very much worse for the wear. The new landscaping design focuses on the hardscape elements such as a fireplace with seating. Decorative elements round out the design, but the location is inhospitable to many common plantings. Instead of greenery, a cleaned brick patio complements a new, bi-panel fence, and an outdoor living room is created with durable furnishings. It's a pulled-together, insightful design that uses the same organizational principles as a galley kitchen.

REGRADE WITH WALLS. Making the most out of a sloped, small yard usually means building retaining walls to create level ground. Terraces create a distinctive look in a relatively tiny amount of space. The interlocking concrete blocks used to make these terraces are easy to install and create a pleasant, durable facade for the landscaped beds. Because you control the culture in each of the terraces (soil acidity, water, etc.), you can mix and match plants to suit your own tastes. The homeowner here created a low-maintenance, low-lying evergreen shrub display that is far more appealing than a sketchy slope of struggling lawn.

LANDSCAPE WITH STRUCTURES. Where your soil or growing conditions are poor, or where you prefer not to deal with a plant-heavy landscape design, you can turn to other materials to fill up a small space. Here, a deck and small reflecting pool take up most of the space in a modest backyard. The designer has used an interesting technique to create visual interest in lieu of varied shapes and hues; a gray background color runs throughout the design, while bright tropical colors are added in the forms of containers, shade sails, and accents. It's a technique that is quite effective in any small space, and one you can use whether you're working with plants or inert materials like the design here.

DIVIDE BUT UNIFY. You can make a medium-sized landscape seem more expansive by breaking it into irregular shapes—something the eye always finds intriguing. The thread that holds this yard design together is a broad strip of brick edging. A long flower garden creates a stunning visual point of separation between the house and lush lawn surface.

REPEAT COLORS FOR A COHESIVE APPEARANCE. There's nothing wrong with an expanse of unbroken lawn in a landscape—just as long as it doesn't stand in for a truly landscaped yard. The richly varied foundation plantings of this landscape provide contrast to the flat green lawn, and include a dynamic mix of shapes that combine to create eye-catching curb appeal. A tree centered in the lawn ensures the emerald patch does not present a boring visual. The red mulch, red leaves and red brick tie the yard elements together.

GET A LITTLE NEGATIVE. "Empty" space, like the arc of grass in this landscape, is an important element in medium landscapes. Not only is a space like this adaptable to many different activities, from cloud-gazing to a game of tag, it also serves the same role as negative or white space does in art; it is a visual pause that provides perspective for the more decorative elements of the raised beds and shrub border in the distance, and small plantings around the patio in the foreground.

CREATE VISUAL MOVEMENT. Giving the eye a logical progression to follow is key to a successful landscape. The curb appeal of this front yard is self-evident, but the reason why it works is less so. The eye begins at a well-defined foreground border along the front edge of the lawn. The border is composed of low, spreading ornamental grasses that give way to the expanse of lawn in the midground. The lawn leads the eye on to beds in the background that give way to the home's facade.

MIRROR IMAGES FRAME A HOME. Symmetry is not necessarily boring, nor is it always a formal look. As the front yard of this brick contemporary home clearly shows, sometimes a symmetrical design is an answer to existing landscape features. Two mature trees stand like sentries in front of the house, so the designer made the most of them by creating island plantings at their bases. Interestingly, the design includes stacked paver borders that complement the the orderly look of the home's brick construction. It's another effective use of contrast in a medium-sized yard.

Before

After

MAKE MAGIC WITH MULTIPLE LEVELS. This two-story beige house lacks design appeal with an unimaginative bed of generic shrubs along a nondescript concrete walkway. The new landscape incorporates a dynamic raised bed, curving pathway between driveway and entrance, and a compelling composition of trees, shrubs, and blooming annuals. Create more drama in a mid-size flat landscape by developing different levels.

MIX HARD ELEMENTS WITH SOFT. A medium-sized front yard is big enough to allow landscaping drama to unfold. The sloped yard in front of this late Victorian-style house has been exploited to the maximum with a broad staircase featuring sweeping curbs, big, overfilled annual beds on either side, and a brick retaining wall holding back another bed. Short brick columns with bowl planters add height. The landscape does not exactly match the architectural style of the home but—more importantly—it does work with it. Don't be afraid to experiment outside the perceived "proper" style.

Large Landscapes

Before

TURN A NEGATIVE INTO A POSITIVE. A large, steep yard may seem like a difficult site on which to design a compelling landscape. A little creative landscaping and some lumberjacking, however, can bring a slope to life. This home stands atop a small hill and the grass slope that ran down to a viewing deck below was hardly an inspired visual. The designer used the slope as a canvas on which to place an amazing assortment of shrubs, trees, and flowering plants. Looking up, the slope is viewed almost as a vertical surface, giving the plantings maximum exposure and visibility. A broad stone staircase and landings look less intimidating surrounded by plantings.

After

Large Landscapes

CHANGE YOUR PERSPECTIVE. This expansive property features a central shrub border ringed by a wide swath of grass. The grass is bordered on the outside by varied and brilliant flowering bushes and perennials, such as the spiky veronica that fronts this bed. The bed also partially conceals a birdbath, evidence of the designer's intention to create a planting attractive to wildlife. The landscape exemplifies two large-area design principles: effective use of unifying negative or empty space (flowing lawn), and a changing vista from any position in the landscape. The view is constantly evolving, making for a fascinating outdoor area.

DRESS UP DREARY ELEMENTS. Define a large front yard with a specimen planting. This can be one of the most effective landscaping techniques. A distinctive tree, such as the one shown here bracketed by boxwood hedges, creates a focal point that uses the rest of the landscape as a stage. The right specimen planting allows you to make the landscape interesting, while limiting the amount of maintenance and upkeep you need to perform.

DRESS UP DREARY ELEMENTS. Embellish pathways through large yards, making the pathway an element for design development. Adding shrubs or borders of lower-growing annuals or perennials reinforces the path's separation from the larger field of lawn. It also creates more visual interest when a simple concrete walkway would have been boring.

CREATE CORNERS. When designing a large landscape, try starting at the corners. Create unique, well-defined areas with their own identities. The island gazebo overlooking this garden pond has a romantic quality that transforms a plain corner into a favorite locale.

THINK INDESTRUCTIBLE. A large yard calls for a spacious pathway that accommodates groups of visitors in comfort if you entertain outdoors quite a bit, hosting large parties and get-togethers. This path is fairly distinctive, not only because it's wide, but also because it reverses the more traditional path design of a wide swath of lawn edged in stone. Here, the crushed yellow stone forms the heart of the path, and thin grass strips clearly delineate the path from the beds on either side.

STOP AND SMELL THE ROSES (AND MARIGOLDS). A flower-strewn landscape creates an incredibly beautiful scene, especially as part of a large landscape. Don't let that beauty—and the effort it takes to create it—go to waste. If you've opted to color your landscape with a profusion of either perennial or annual flowers, as the designer did here, add a seating area where all that gorgeous color can be enjoyed.

Landscape Plantings

Plants are often thought of as synonymous with landscaping. Say the word *landscaping* and most people think of massed walls of greenery, long stretches of well-tended lawn, and clusters of flowering plants. Although features such as waterfalls and pools, statuary, and hardscaping sometimes steal the attention, most landscapes rely on vegetation for at least background support to the design.

Plants are, however, just as eligible to be the stars of the show. The right Japanese maple or dogwood tree in the right location can be a fantastic addition to a landscape design. A trellis cloaked in climbing roses, or a wall draped in morning glory or passionflower vines, is an endlessly fascinating sight. Even the more moderate mixed bed of blooming annuals and perennials can be color fireworks.

The vast range of plant types means there is one perfect for whatever space you need to fill. A shrub border is a typical foundation planting, but you can fill it out with sprawling and spreading evergreens in shades from blue-gray to bright lime green. Or fill the border along a shady pathway with rhododendron over a collection of different hostas for a dozen shades of green and seasonal purple, pink, or white blossoms. The possibilities are nearly endless.

CHOOSE PLANTS YOU LIKE. It might seem obvious, but most of us like things for the same reasons, so sticking to plants you respond to is a good indicator that they will go together well. Here, a medium-height tree provides a pleasing canopy, while evergreen shrubs dot the yard with spots of year-round life. Other flowering plants are positioned throughout to supply intriguing warm colors just about anywhere the eye might wander. There's even a small lawn to provide a visual pause in what is a symphony of flora.

USE PLANTS TO SOFTEN HARD LINES. Contrast is one of the more powerful tools in the landscaping toolbox. Taking advantage of this slope meant terracing it with borders of stacked fieldstone. It would have been easy to plant the terraced beds with groundcovers or sprawling evergreens, but filling them with a tumble of blooming annuals creates a spectacular contrast between hard and soft, rigid and flowing, and bursts of color against the neutral hues of the stone.

Whichever you choose, plants are a changeable part of any landscape—a fact that makes them the most interesting and most challenging element in designing your landscape. Think ahead and try to envision how plantings will look in every season and as they mature over the years. Seasonal bloomers, such as bulbs, will be easier to design into the landscape than a shrub that presents a different look every season. One thing's certain—cultivate the right plants in the right location and you'll add dynamite to your landscape.

BUILD A CURVED BED NEXT TO A STRAIGHT FENCE OR WALL. Curving garden beds are almost always a great look for the landscape (the exception being in highly formal and linear landscapes). Raised beds allow you to control the culture of what you plant because you can adjust soil pH and nutrients according to the needs of the plants. This particular bed boasts some excellent design elements, including trios of plants, a well-designed fence that contrasts but does not fight for attention with the shape and material of the bed, and a wonderful mix of colors that will change throughout the year.

USE A CURVED BED TO DIVIDE OPEN SPACE. Raised garden beds, such as the curving stacked flagstone beds shown here, are a great way to create crisp definition between a lawn and garden. The bed containers themselves offer another chance to add mightily to the decorative appeal of the landscape. Use wood, stone, or brick to contain a raised bed—depending on which material best suits the look of your landscape. A raised bed like this also serves a practical purpose, keeping lawn fertilizer and weed killer from infiltrating the bed soil and harming garden plants.

SMALL TREES ARE A GOOD FIT IN PLANTING BEDS. If you're the low-maintenance type, consider the sort of mixed tree and shrub bed the designer created for this landscape spot. Dominated by two dwarf Japanese maples, the bed is filled with lower growing green and red foliage plants in a lovely mix of leaf shapes. The basic muted reds and greens are not only perfectly complementary, they also pop against the darker background of the evergreen forest that borders the property. It's a masterly composition, eloquent in its simplicity.

DON'T IGNORE SHADED AREAS. This dense rich bed offers a wealth of shape, mass, and texture, along with about one hundred shades of green. The spot is a deep shade area with less than ideal drainage. However, a little time spent investigating what's on offer at the local nursery will lead you to many great shade plants that will thrive for months and provide dense greenery such as this— the perfect answer to the shadowy challenges in your landscape.

USE CONTAINERS FOR CONSTANT VARIETY. A love of flowers drives this design, which features a concrete circular patio looking out over a rose garden and bed of mixed flowers, and vegetables blended in so that they are part of the design. The beds are a contrast to the orderly, trim, tidy look of the lawn and the sculpted hedges bordering the patio. Container plantings allow for changeable displays. When incorporating containers into your design, consider the technique used here—repetitive color and shape that keeps the area from looking too haphazard.

CREATE A LIVING BORDER. Low-growing flowering annuals, such as the pink impatiens that line the edge of this shrub bed, are a spectacular choice for edging. Choose plants that grow with a mounding or bush-like habit and they will not only add vibrant color, they'll also provide mass that creates effective visual transition up from the flat surface of the lawn, to the rounded shapes of the shrubs behind.

PERENNIALS OFFER BIG COLOR WITH LITTLE WORK. Perennial borders are low-maintenance options where you want plenty of reliable color year after year. This particular planting includes the ever-popular black-eyed Susan and sedum. The designer has taken care to include not only a stunning mix of colors, but also a variety of flower and foliage shapes and heights. Variety is the spice of life when it comes to flowering beds and borders. Don't neglect the nose when putting together your flowering displays; the phlox used here is mildly fragrant, but plants like honeysuckle and roses are even more so.

INVEST IN A CUTTING GARDEN. A cut-flower garden offers a double bounty: stunning hues for the landscape and impressive floral displays for inside the house. This cut-flower bed includes a diversity of flowers, from tall to short and sprawling, providing blooms from late spring through early fall. Mixing species is a great way to create dynamic visual appeal in a flower bed, ensuring that you have color for as long as possible.

Using Shrubs, Trees, and Vines

Before

After

WORK OUTWARD FROM THE FOUNDATION. This landscape was flat and unvarying with no relief between the bare lawn and the distinctive stone and brick house. A simple foundation planting of shrubs in various shapes and sizes softens the straight lines and hard surfaces of the house and complements the unusual winding pathway leading from the driveway to the front door.

DON'T MAKE A TREE FLY SOLO. A simple shrub bed around the base of a mature tree builds mass up to the vertical trunk embellishes a fairly plain landscape feature. One the great things about a shrub bed like this is that you can experiment with trimming the shrubs or letting them grow and blend naturally

ENJOY THE PEAK BUT HAVE AN ALL-SEASONS PLAN. A specimen planting is a surefire way to show off any stunning flowering tree—or any unusually distinctive plant—to its best advantage. Here, a flowering cherry tree provides an incredible show of pink blossoms. Even when the blooms fade, the tree will leaf out into a handsome full canopy. In colder months, the form of the branches and the gnarled trunk will still supply plenty of visual interest. Notice the blooming groundcover, which was selected to complement the signature pink of the cherry blossoms.

BALANCE A TREE CANOPY WITH BASE PLANTINGS. That's why it's a common design practice to dress up the base of a tree. The island planting around this tree trunk includes a wealth of flowers and a border that takes its cue from the brick facade of the house. It's a bed where the eye doesn't expect to see one, and adds immensely to the appeal of the tree. Use this technique whenever you want to add yard-level interest around a medium to large tree.

MAKE YOUR PLANTING BEDS MOVE. This simple bed is actually a study in basic landscape design. The bed masses upward from the door to an inside corner. The shrub in back is perfectly matched to the engaging forms of ornamental grasses up front. The short trees will mature—a fact that the designer took into account by placing the tree on the left so it would not block window views.

USE SHRUBS TO FRAME LANDSCAPE OR HOUSE FEATURES. A simple modern take on the formal garden fills this small backyard with a design that is at once sophisticated and inviting. The shrubs in the design are used sparingly, filling out the garden and providing rounded shapes that contrast the neat lines of the center courtyard. The shrubs are shaped as they would be in a strictly formal design, giving the whole look a soft, gentle appeal.

KEEP YOUR SHRUBS NEAT AND TRIM. Neatly trimmed shrubs are one of the key indicators of a formal approach to a landscape design. The arbor vitae that line the back fence in this yard are no exception, looking like a row of perfect sentinels standing guard. Be careful when shaping shrubs to affect a formal appearance or even just to create a fun shape; you have to be sure the form does not block sun from reaching the bottom part of the shrub.

Using Shrubs, Trees, and Vines

KEEP TREES AND SHRUBS BALANCED. Combining trees and shrubs in close proximity creates mass, a crucial part of any landscape design. Areas of mass are often superimposed against "empty" areas such as the swath of lawn that runs between these two beds. This creates intriguing visual depth and balances the visual weight of the landscape. The balance of open space, trees, and shrubs prevents the yard from feeling too enclosed but also creates an impression of rich fullness.

CREATE A CATHEDRAL OF VINES. A classic vine like wisteria—although it can resemble a tree or large shrub as it matures—is one of the most beautiful and evocative climbers you can incorporate into a landscape. They are most often draped over arbors, archways, or as it is here, along a pergola that stands alongside a ground-level deck. One of the wonderful things about wisteria is that even after the blooms are gone, the twisted, crooked, and knobby trunk is still eye-catching. You can do a lot worse than using this vine where you want a stunning, long-lasting eye-catcher in your landscape.

EXPLOIT THE ARCHITECTURAL QUALITIES OF PLANTS. Shrubs such as the arbor vitae on either side of this entryway are ideal to emphasize vertical lines. Here, the tall shrubs are used to contrast the horizontal lines of a row of boxwood shrubs, and the foliage and flowering groundcovers that front the stone wall. Notice the ivy growing up the stone pillars; ivy can soften the appearance of hard surfaces, but it requires caution in landscaping. Many types of ivy are invasive and and some can degrade surfaces, including masonry and wood.

KEEP TREES AND SHRUBS IN LINE. Espalier is a technique that allows the landscape designer or homeowner to use trees as a fence. The trees (in this case, apple trees along the long wall of a cobbled courtyard) are trained and pruned to form a living barricade. Here, the technique is used decoratively, as a stunning stand-in for a long plain white courtyard wall. The roses on the far wall are being trained to the shape of arching trellis, adding even more decorative interest to what would otherwise be a charming but very plain space.

Surfaces and Pathways

As far as modern landscaping goes, the bare concrete slab has gone the way of the nickel loaf of bread. There's no rule against using concrete for outdoor surfaces, and it is certainly still being incorporated in new and innovative ways, but the options are so much more plentiful than an undistinguished poured surface.

Using natural materials is a great way to link pathways, patios, and other structures to the vegetation in your landscape. Most often this means stone in one of its many beautiful forms. The type of stone you choose should be based upon the look you're after. A broken flagstone floor is informal, rugged and charming. If your landscape is more regimented, you may prefer to turn to cut stone pavers or slate tiles for their crisp appearance and the ease with which they can be laid.

However, the durable materials collectively known as "hardscaping" aren't your only landscaping surface options. Aside from making a wonderful lawn, grass can be used for pathways and as borders or accents in a patio. Other soft surfaces, such as chipped or shredded wood, can also stand in for stone or concrete. Often, these softer materials are combined with hardscape to create truly intriguing pathways or patios.

Practical considerations play a big part in the material you'll choose for landscape surfaces and structures such as steps or walls. Chief among these

MAKE A STRONG STATEMENT WITH SURFACES. There are basically two different ways to use hardscaping in your landscape design: as a complement to focal points, or as a focal point. An intricately designed outdoor floor such as the one shown here can set the motif for the landscape (for instance, repetitive circle shapes in beds, plantings and water features), but keep in mind that this a permanent design element. The concrete ring and varied paver directions and shapes of this surface were carefully thought out. Work hardscape designs like this out on paper first, with accurate measurements, before you ever break ground.

COMBINE PATHWAY MATERIALS. Combination pathways are an interesting variant that you should consider if the path is long and wide. Generally, the combination involves a bed of fine particles—such as the crushed stone in this path—with solid steps set into the infill. Combination paths usually have some type of border that helps define and shape the path and keeps the infill in place. A word of caution, though: heavier infill is often the better choice because lighter materials such as wood chips and bark have a habit of quickly spreading beyond the borders of the path.

FLAGSTONE: NATURE'S JIGSAW PUZZLE. Flagstone is one of the most common landscape paving materials; the term actually describes a variety of stones formed in the same way. That variety accounts for differences in appearance that range from blue to gray to nearly white to muted red. But all have a fairly uneven irregular surface texture that prevents the stones from becoming too slippery when wet.

is cost. Depending on how large the surface area is that you want to cover, material prices may limit the options. In most cases, though, a modest pathway or small patio will not eat up a lot of your budget regardless of the paving you choose.

Other issues to consider when putting down a new surface include drainage and how slick the material will be when wet. This is especially important for any outdoor floor around a pool, spa tub, or other water feature.

With due consideration given to practical concerns, begin designing your outdoor surfaces. In general, a patio or pathway is a chance to add interesting shapes and textures to the landscape. Remember that straight lines are considered a formal and restrained look. Contrary to conventional wisdom, they are rarely the quickest way to connect the two "points" represented by your current yard and the ideal landscape you envision.

Hardscape Paths

ASHLAR is a quarried stone with a plain appearance, ideal for pathways that are simply utilitarian or where the hardscaping needs to complement bolder elements in the design. It's inexpensive and easy to work with, and usually sold smooth-cut into large bricks that can be used in garden walls as well.

FIELDSTONE got its name from the fact that this plentiful material is found for the taking in fields, dry riverbeds, and hillsides. The stones can be cut to create a flat face for pathways, although is sometimes partially sunk in its natural form, as rounded stepping stones in a naturalist, informal landscape design. Fieldstone is also widely used in landscape walls and steps.

COBBLESTONES are a traditional garden paving choice, and reclaimed types often have beautiful surfaces that make a path or patio a standout surface. New or old, they give the landscape a charming, old-world feel.

CRUSHED STONE is a cruder version of pea gravel. It also comes in various sizes small to large and is created through natural or mechanical means. However, almost all crushed stone is jagged and, therefore, not ideal for any surface that might see barefoot traffic. The material is a great low-cost mulch substitute in xeriscaped designs.

DECOMPOSED GRANITE is attractive and not as jagged as crushed stone. It makes wonderful infill in a path or patio that features large stone or wood insets. The gritty, sandy texture can stick to shoes, so it's not ideal for surfaces that lead directly into a house.

PEA GRAVEL sees a great deal of use in landscaping, as a crude fill material that can be compacted to allow for drainage and as a base for another hardscape, or as a pathway or patio material itself. The gravel is created by mechanical or natural crushing and is sold in different sizes and as jagged or smooth stones. Smooth pea gravel is used as infill for paths and patios and comes in shades of gray, white, and yellow—the white and yellow are the colors most often used for landscape surfaces.

RIVER ROCKS are larger, smooth stones that are sold in many different sizes, but all have smooth surfaces. They are available in a mix of white, grays, and browns. Smaller sizes create attractive paths and even patios (the smaller the river rock, the more comfortable it is to walk on). Larger versions are nice accents under sculpture, ornaments, and around specimen plantings. Polished river rock and pebbles are decorative versions. The stones are polished to an enchanting shiny finish that looks great in path or under sculpture or ornaments.

NATURAL FLAGSTONE is cleft into slabs with irregular shapes and an often interesting, flaky top surface. Flagstone is also available in precut tiles.

CREATE A VANISHING POINT. One of the most effective devices in designing a path through landscaping is to create a "vanishing point" so that the termination of the path cannot be seen from either end. This creates intriguing visual depth and mystery—hallmarks of great landscape design. It's an especially effective technique to use with a hardscaped path such as the brick surface here, because the path tends to stand out visually from the surrounding surface.

INTRODUCE THE UNEXPECTED. Landscape paths are the perfect place to introduce the unexpected into your design. The more the path surprises someone strolling along it, the more fun it brings to the design. Here, stepping stones have been set on foundations to "float" across the water of a pond. It's an intriguing look that fools the eye and creates a delightful element. You can use the same effect in crossing from one surface to another, such as running stepping stones across a lawn and then onto a low deck. But use care to avoid any surprises that may be dangerous.

EXPLOIT YOUR MATERIALS—EVEN THE HUMBLE ONES. Concrete might not be the most popular surface material for landscaping, but it still can play a valuable role in the right place and situation. Here, a winding front walkway was easily laid, with two shrub beds lining either side. The concrete serves as negative space between the busy colorful plantings, breaking them up and helping emphasize the variety and beauty of the plants.

EMBRACE NATURAL BEAUTY. Stone slabs make for a wonderfully rustic look in a pathway. It's not hard to design a simple path like the one shown here, although the slabs can be a challenge to move around. One of the wonderful things about slabs is that they can be overlapped, as shown in this path, to form natural and attractive steps.

Hardscape Paths

BALANCE CONTRAST AND SCALE. Although the look is more regimented and formal than you might expect to find in a wild native landscape, it works in this landscape for a couple of reasons. The color of the brick walkway is actually the perfect complementary hue to the green of the lawn. The walkway also creates a brushstroke across the landscape that sharply contrasts the other irregular shapes and earth tones. If the walkway were any larger, that contrast would jar the eye. As it is, the contrast sets up engaging visual tension. When and if you work with contrasts in your landscape, limit their scope to ensure the effect doesn't overwhelm the whole design.

NEAT PREFERS NEAT. Trim, neat, and well-sculpted landscape plantings beg for a hardscape surface that echoes those qualities. This brick bridge between the asphalt of a circular driveway and the slate of the entryway is an alluring creamy red that is just understated enough to work with all the plants surrounding the front door. It's also a great way to transition from the undistinguished appearance of the driveway, to the elegant mottled gray of the front steps.

DIRT IS THE ORIGINAL HARDSCAPE. Don't overlook the ground itself as hardscape. As this outdoor staircase shows, compacted earth can serve as steps or a patio. A specifically unique treatment, the steps here are formed by level stretches of ground separated by nosings of buried stones. It's a very cool look, reminiscent of Zen gardens and landscapes.

PAY ATTENTION TO PATTERNS. Mortared brick makes a beautiful and permanent surface in the landscape, one that is classic and timeless. A form such as this path and brick patio requires a good deal of planning to ensure the brick patterns work well with other lines in the landscape. If you decide on a brick path, make sure that you purchase bricks meant as pavers—other types may crack and heave under the forces of a freeze-thaw cycle.

Hardscape Paths

LET EDGE PLANTINGS CREEP IN. Cut flagstone makes for clearly defined paths. These types of hard-line geometric walkways usually work best when they are bordered by plantings that will at least slightly overgrow the edges of the path, as they do everywhere in this landscape. Not only do the plants soften the look of the hard lines, they also pleasantly brush anyone walking by, adding to the tactile enjoyment of a garden. Don't be afraid to plant flowers or shrubs close to the edge of a hardscaped path such as this.

USE INSERTS TO BREAK UP HOMOGENOUS SURFACES. A clever way to integrate a hardscape patio or path with the surrounding landscape vegetation is to break it up with a living insert. Here, the planted square is accented with a red urn, but you can use a spot like this to show off a specimen plant such as a dwarf maple or cherry tree. A large container overflowing with plants will serve almost the same role on a long or large hardscape surface.

GET PLAYFUL AT THE FRINGES. If the path is not meant to be used as a regular avenue of travel, you can get more creative—some would even say funky—with the design of the path. Here, a slab path in an out-of-the-way corner of the garden leads to what seems like a wonderful secret spot full of rich color. The slabs have been placed at odd angles and the flowering perennials and annuals have been planted in a seemingly random pattern. It makes the whole corner of this garden look like a happy accident. The truth is, this kind of design takes a lot of planning and work, but the look is definitely worth it! But take care not to create a path that is unsafe.

STACK IT AND FORGET IT. Need a long staircase up a hill or steep slope? Turn to slabs. Slabs make natural steps, they are easy to configure, and once you set them in place, they usually stay there. The downside to working with slabs is the heavy, cumbersome stone pieces, but your effort will pay off in the long run because they last a long time and look great for that entire span.

Hardscape Paths

CURB YOUR ENTHUSIASM. Add curbstones as the icing on the cake of formal paths. The curbstones here clearly demarcate the borders of this straight path, and give it an even more orderly look. Curbstones also serve a useful function of keeping soil from eroding out of garden beds. Depending on the pavers you're using in your path, you can simply lay them on edge or end to create a curb, or use actual granite curbstones as the designer has done here.

PIT SHAPE AGAINST FORM. Mix formal and informal path elements to create riveting landscape highways that hold as much visual interest as the surrounding plantings. Large square cut pavers have been set in the ground through this overgrown landscape, to create a well-defined path. Loose infill of pea gravel surrounds the squares. It's a captivating visual mix that includes sharp geometric forms within an indistinct border—and it wasn't hard to create! Note the small globes that dot the edges of the pathway.

STEPPING STONES COMPEL YOU TO FOLLOW. Use stepping stones to make some of the most compelling paths in the landscape. Although this is an informal look, it's also very inviting—there is something about a series of stepping stones that leads the traveler through a landscape setting. Adding infill between the steps is a time-tested technique that makes a stepping-stone path even more engaging. The look here is stunning, and contrasts the hard, sharp edges of the stepping stones with the rounded organic shapes of river rocks.

WHEN IN DOUBT, BE NATURAL. Stone steps blend natural elegance and beauty for a stunning landscape feature in any yard. Depending on how stylized the design is and the type of stone (natural shaped or cut square), the steps can enhance either a formal or casual outdoor living area.

STRAIGHT LINES CAN TAKE INTERESTING TURNS. As shown here, you can still add a lot of visual variety as the path makes its way from point A to point B. The key is to vary the width of the path along its course, and create offshoots that lend a sense of mystery and possibility. This zigzag path is as intriguing as any curved landscape avenue would be, and still maintains the orderly design perspective lines naturally bring to the landscape

A FORK IN THE PATHWAY CAN PROVOKE. Amplify the enchanting effect of stepping stones embedded across a lawn by splitting the path. This technique creates even more mystery and intrigue in the landscape design. The visitor has two paths to take, which raises questions and draws attention to different areas within a landscape, such as a pond and a specimen planting. You can use this technique with straight pathways as well.

CAST YOUR OWN CUSTOM CONCRETE PAVERS. Always look to leapfrog creative ideas off of old landscape design standards for unique and effective pathway appearances. The idea of a path made from hardscape pavers embedded in loose infill is taken a step farther here; the designer has used concrete circular pavers, with a stamped design, arranged along a path of low-growing groundcover plants.

MAKE A RIVER OF RIVER ROCK. Whenever possible, use common landscaping materials in uncommon ways. Pathways are some of the best opportunities to do this, as this one clearly illustrates. The designer has created a broad, level surface with bleached, smooth, large river rocks. It's an unusual look, and all the more eye-catching for being unusual.

HEDGES CAN TURN A PATHWAY INTO A HARDWAY. Create even more allure on a landscape by exploiting the sense of mystery contained within tunnels and passageways. The designer here has used "walls" of tall shrubs along either side of an informal stepping stone pathway, creating a look that would be right at home in an enchanted garden. Although you could create this effect with manmade structures such as fences, use shrubs or clusters of trees to design a truly naturalistic look.

Soft-Surface Paths

A RIBBON OF LAWN FEELS NICE UNDERFOOT. Used as it is here, the relationship of grass to yard seems reversed from what we've come to expect. A sprawling landscape strewn with a mix of shrubs and ornamental grasses is bisected by a ribbon of neatly tended lawn. It's an excellent and witty addition to the scene, and a great way to add a walkway through any informal bed or landscape. However, be aware that the crisp edges and velvety surface of this path come at a price: it demands a lot more maintenance than hardscaped surfaces.

A WIDE PATH HAS ROOM TO WANDER. A wide, generous swath of lawn serves as both a walkway and a viewing platform for a stunning mixed bed of trees and shrubs. Although it's tempting to make all paths through the landscape quaint and unique, the main passageways should be broad enough to accommodate several people (think garden party or cookout) and plain enough to serve as a foil for the rest of the landscape. This arching walkway fills the bill in both respects.

A 50/50 SPLIT HAS POSITIVE TENSION. As this informal walkway clearly shows, grass, moss, or even low-growing groundcovers are perfect partners to harder materials underfoot. The mix of random stone slabs scattered among grass is greater than the sum of its parts. This is a way to make any path completely unique and utterly interesting. The monocolor border featuring a flourish of annuals completes an amazing picture.

PATHWAYS LOVE A PUNCTUATION MARK One way to make a straight path pay off is to point it at a distinctive landscape feature you're looking to showcase. In this garden, the path leads directly to a sculptured specimen tree that stands out in the surrounding tumble of flowering plants. The path is bordered with cobblestones, which not only adds to the European old-world look, but also provides a very practical mowing strip that keeps the grass from invading the flowerbeds and vice versa. Using grass as a path provides comfort underfoot, and complements the terminating focal point—it's a great principle to embrace if you want to use a straight path in your garden.

A CIRCULAR BRICK DESIGN MAKES A TRULY STUNNING PATIO. The clay paving bricks used here are neutral toned, leaving the circular pattern and central tree ring to hog the attention. Circular and curving paver patterns are informal and visually engaging, especially when the circular pattern radiates from a center focal point as it does here. Notice how the unstructured shapes and soft forms of the abundant plant life surrounding the patio create a nearly seamless continuity between the patio and the surrounding landscape.

CAST CONCRETE PAVERS MIMIC TRADITIONAL LOOKS. Cobblestone pavers offer some of the most unique appearances among hardscape materials. Older cobblestones have an attractive mottled appearance that you can exploit by arranging the stones to their best advantage. New, replica cobblestones like the ones shown here are set in sand. The brick-shaped stones used in the edging add a nice finished touch to the surface. Special edging treatments are a way to add a unique look to any hardscaped floor.

LOOSE FILL HAS MANY PLUSSES. Materials such as crushed stone, pea gravel, or shredded wood can make a casual, useful patio surface. This type of material can also be installed much easier than stone surfaces, and requires virtually no upkeep. The nature of the material ensures that spilled beverages and food won't stain the surface and aren't a big issue to clean up. That's why loose infill is great for outdoor dining areas, as it's used in this yard. However, it's wise to use solid edging (wood strips here) to corral the material and prevent it from migrating into adjacent lawns and garden beds.

PATCHES OF GRASS HAVE A COOLING EFFECT. These squares actually carry through the geometric theme that is established with the shape of the pool and spa tub, and the outlines of the lawn itself. It's a fairly unique "controlled" approach that creates a lovely, sophisticated look. Some, such as these large concrete squares interspersed in a lawn, are more like outdoor floors but can provide all the benefits of a patio.

COMPARTMENTALIZE YOUR PATIO. Even in a small or medium-sized yard, it's simply good design to break up sitting areas. Here, a crescent of grass invites barefoot living, a colored concrete main patio serves as a place for drinks and dinner, and a corner pergola provides a shady respite, separate but still linked with the rest of the landscape.

ADD A BUMP-OUT TO A WALKWAY. Here, a long, thin side yard is made eminently useful with the aid of two paver pathways that meet and mingle in a small patio. The placement of the square flagstones, both in the paths and patio, seems very organic and natural. The plants appear to have grown around the hard surfaces almost by happenstance. Never shy from odd corners of your yard—properly designed, they can host wonderful getaway spaces, like the patio shown here.

STICK WITH A STYLE. The slate outdoor floor in this Japanese style yard is a perfect example. Different shapes and sizes of tiles combine with details such as "slots" filled with polished river rocks that really stand out. It's a stunning surface that provides both a place to sit and admire the rest of the landscape and a focal point in its own right. Work a design like this out on paper to make the actual process of laying the surface quicker and easier.

EXPLOIT NEW MATERIALS. This elevated patio is created using interlocking blocks that essentially come in a kit. In a lofty spot, a hardscape patio is less likely to have drainage problems. Elevating a landscaping surface such as this gives it a better view over standout features, such as the small pond that has been built into the side of the patio. As a bonus, the level of the patio creates an ideal walk-in surface for the spa tub.

BUILD AN EXOTIC GROTTO. There are alternatives to laying a patio, and decking is one of the most common. However, it's popular to build huge decks that dominate and overwhelm the landscape design. Here, the opposite has been done. This step-up deck is used as a centerpiece to a jungle landscape, where the homeowners can dine and relax Asian-style in dappled sunlight amid verdant surroundings.

SMALL SCALE = ROMANTIC. Crowded by plants all around and positioned next to a lattice screen and pergola, this small sitting area provides of bit of negative space in the busy tumble of plants. Design-wise, it serves the same purpose as a pause in a piece of music. It's also a very intimate and relaxing spot, where the rest of the world seems a million miles away.

CHOOSE THE BEST SPOT FOR A REMOTE PATIO. Like all real estate, "location, location, location" is key to great patio and landscape design. Where your yard is wide open and the patio could be sited just about anywhere, always consider sun exposure in your decision. The patio here was positioned to have a perfect view of the sunset on summer afternoons and full sun exposure at other times. You can decide whether full sun or shade suits your lifestyle better, but make it a conscious decision when designing a patio into your landscape plan.

CONCRETE CAN BE BEAUTIFUL. This patio is stunning, with concrete squares featuring a pebbly, exposed-aggregate surface, and a superimposed brick grid. The hard surface and the color contrasts everything around the patio and, like a body of water, it provides clear separation and effective negative space that gives the surrounding plants more visual power. You can do a lot with a concrete patio by playing with its surface appearance, from dying the material a different color, to impressing designs into the wet concrete with metal or plastic stamps.

PATIOS LOVE WALLS. A natural position for a hardscaped patio is up against a garden wall. Position the surface as it has been here, to give the patio a visual anchor in the landscape. In many cases, the garden wall naturally shades the patio for at least part of the day. As with other structures in the landscape that abut one another, it helps if you include transition plantings, such as the low shrubs that line the seam between the patio and timber wall in this landscape.

DESIGN A COURTYARD AS A CONVERSATION PIT. Adapt to the size and configuration of the space you have to work with. This tiny townhouse courtyard presented a big challenge to the designer; the answer was to provide visual interest by blending surface textures and adding splashes of plant life. A trellis supports vines hardy enough to grow in the low-light situation, and a hardscape patio design mixes with a more flowing deck design to make this one lovely—if modest—outdoor spot.

TAKE A STEP DOWN TO OUTDOOR LIVING. Sunken patios can be incredible features when used in the right place. Here, a sunken brick patio is positioned with a large rock face as a background. Nesting a sunken surface in this way creates a sense of intimacy—a feeling that is reinforced in this Asian-inspired design with thick growth on all sides, and overhanging branches. The key issue when adding a sunken outdoor floor to your landscape is drainage. Ensure the area drains well and establish a solid bed for the hardscape surface, and the patio will remain dry and stable over the long run.

CHOOSE FURNISHINGS THAT REFLECT YOUR THEME. Tropical plants make the look authentic, but so does the appropriate hardscape surface. The crudely textured square pavers used for this patio resemble lava rock and its associations with volcanic island paradises. The ornate Indonesian-style furniture helps drive the theme home.

USE ELEMENTS FROM YOUR LANDSCAPE TO FASHION FURNISHINGS. Hardscape materials can also make for great seating as this slate and flagstone bench overlooking a pond clearly illustrate. You can create a more formal-looking bench— or individual seating—by stacking cut pavers in an exacting geometric pattern. Keep the seating as low as possible while still comfortable to ensure structural integrity.

THINK OF PATIOS AS ROOM ADDITIONS. Patios attached to a wall of the house, such as this semicircular surface, are highly effective for a number of different reasons. Using a flowing shape like this creates a visual transition from the hard lines of the house to the curves of the garden. A house wall also serves as an excellent starting point for laying the pavers. Located this close to the indoor rooms, the patio is easily served by the kitchen, which makes serving drinks and food outdoors that much simpler.

REPEAT BUILDING MATERIALS IN YOUR PATIO. When the façade of the house is brick, brick patios are a great way to visually tie the patio to the home. This lovely get-away-from-it-all area was dressed up with a privacy fence that, along with lush plantings of trees and shrubs, creates a private, restful retreat. The fence is topped with special flower-filled planters designed to perch on the top rail. Embellish your fences or other structures in this way to blend them into the landscape and enrich the atmosphere around your hardscaped surface.

MAKE PLANS FOR CONTROLLING TRAFFIC ▶

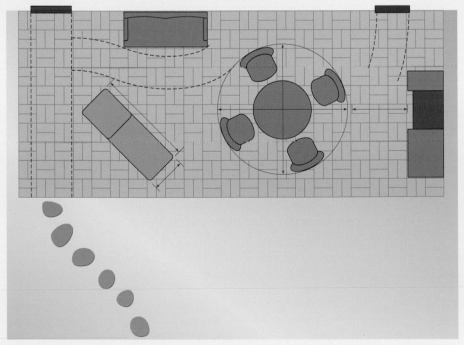

No matter what hardscape material you use, design your patio to accommodate traffic flow and furniture placement. Know how you want people to navigate the surface, what you hope to do on it, and where you want different functions focused. Lanes of travel across a patio should be at least 22 inches wide, and the wider the better. As this diagram shows, you also need to leave working room around grills and sufficient space for chairs to be slid out from around a table, and the correct spacing between furnishings and features.

MAKE A BACKYARD SANCTUARY. Create a cozy outdoor nook by surrounding a small patio area with a horseshoe-shaped low wall. The dry-stacked flagstone wall here is enchanting in its own right, but closes off this patio peninsula to create a feeling of intimacy. That feel is reinforced by plantings that grow higher than the wall. The wall can also serve as additional seating or a place for food and drinks. The designer has added an interesting feature: a V cutout in the middle of the wall that acts like a peephole into the plant life on the other side.

Patios and Courtyards

TAKE A TIP FROM TILE SCHEMES. A well-thought-out hardscape surface design can be endlessly fascinating. This patio incorporates two different types of hardscape: cut flagstone paving slabs and pebbled concrete. The design of the patio defines the center area with a pebbled arc, and a spotlight circle has been designed to focus on a table right in the center. Pavers in the path leading away from the surface are laid out to form arrows pointing away from the patio, and the outdoor kitchen on the other side has been built using the same stone, effectively integrating it into the patio.

SEATING CAN TURN A WIDE WALKWAY INTO A SMALL PATIO. A straight bond brick pattern is as basic as it gets, and the linear shapes shown here are easy to lay out. But more importantly, a basic brick surface such as this is the perfect complement to a formal landscape design. It follows the proliferation of straight lines and geometric forms set by the trimmed plants and adds a solid color that serves as a foil to the plant colors. It's a safe bet to match your hardscape to the landscape style you've chosen.

TREAT YOUR PATIO AS A DESTINATION. Mix hardscape surfaces throughout a large landscape for maximum variety and visual interest. This large yard includes deep, poured concrete steps with fieldstone borders; a formal paver patio; and a packed-earth pathway, all within view of each other. It's a dynamic mix and one that adds to the overall visual punch of this already varied terrain.

CREATE A CENTERPIECE FOR YOUR PATIO. The designer has created an intriguing cross design of formal paving bricks combined with squares of river rocks and added fun visual elements to the point of intersection. The blend of formal lines and informal curved shapes creates an arresting effect. Always consider more than one material if you intend on creating a showcase, one-of-kind patio or courtyard surface.

MATCH YOUR MATERIALS TO YOUR NEEDS. The owner of this yard wanted a patio to sit under a broad, extensive arbor with fine detailing. Loose fill or an irregular surface such as broken flagstone pavers probably would not have supplied the appropriate support for such a large overhead structure, but most certainly wouldn't have matched the style of the arbor. The brick surface does, and it complements the wealth of highly designed plantings as well. Remember that your hardscape patio has to meet your practical needs and aesthetic goals.

THINK OF YOUR LANDSCAPE AS A TAPESTRY. This awe-inspiring surface is the latter. The patio includes a peninsula that bridges a backyard pond. One end of the patio is dominated by a vine-draped arbor, while the rest of the landscape plantings encroach on the surface, from the tree leaning over it, to the spillover from beds front and back. Design your patio to be this integrated with the landscape and you'll make it look as if it has been there forever.

DEFY CONVENTION. "Exposed aggregate" concrete surfacing allows large pieces used in the mixing of material to float to the surface, creating a varied texture. Although this is usually done with small particles such as pea gravel, you can use large river rocks, as the designer of this patio has done. The pebbled surface is pleasant on bare feet and extremely attractive.

Pathways and Transitions

MAKE YOUR PATIO A BIRD SANCTUARY. Place a birdbath on a hardscape surface in a landscape frequented by creatures such as cats and raccoons. The bare expanse of a patio may not seem like the most natural location for a birdbath, but it actually provides protection for the birds because any potential predators are exposed as soon as they try to attack. Use a non-stone birdbath, such as the elegant iron version shown here, to create an interesting contrast with the hardscape and make the feature stand out more.

USE ORDINARY MATERIALS IN UNUSUAL WAYS. Preformed concrete slabs may not appeal to your sense of natural materials, but they can be extremely useful in a landscape design. They come in many different styles, including the exposed aggregate type (shown here), colored versions, and those with the surface stamped with a relief design. They also come in various sizes and uniform shapes. You can use them as you would any paver, or design a more creative surface.

CHOOSE PERMANENT MATERIALS FOR PATIO KITCHENS. Use mortared or otherwise secured paving methods to ensure a stable surface for defined activities like this. The surface texture of flagstones makes non-slippery for outdoor entertaining, even when wet. Use mortared surfaces—rather than loose, irregular pavers—around hot tubs, dining areas and other high-traffic patio features.

Pathways and Transitions

LOOSE GRAVEL FOLLOWS ANY FORM. The path here is a clear example of how once the material is captured by edging, it looks extremely neat and contrasts with the plant life. Gravel also inexpensive and easy to install but is not necessarily pleasant on bare feet—less of an issue in front yards than in back.

DON'T BE A SQUARE. Unusual outline shapes make a patio much more interesting than it might otherwise be—in terms of the entire landscape design. The rectangle-with-cutout design shown here suits the landscaping perfectly, but the really intriguing element of this hardscaping is the subtle change in levels, giving the impression of a flat surface layered over another flat surface. It's a sophisticated look you can use on almost any hardscaped transition area, pathway or patio. The technique works best with precise geometric shapes.

NOT ALL WHO WANDER ARE LOST. Even when you intend the path to go directly from one point or another, try to give a stepping stone walkway a meandering quality, as the designer of this path has done. The romantic quality of the irregular steps belies the careful placement that is the hallmark of an effective path design. Notice the wonderful touch the designer added at the border of the bed and the grass, where a sprinkling of stepping stones breaks from the pattern before resuming into a path again. Small touches such as this have big visual impact in an irregular hardscape pathway.

Landscape Walls and Steps

WALL MATERIALS ▶

Garden walls can be built from many different materials. Choose stone based on whether you want a cut-stone look (ashlar and interlocking concrete blocks are the most common), the regular geometry and traditional reds of a brick surface, or the rounded, irregular and casual appearance of uncut-fieldstone wall—dry laid or mortared. You can use concrete blocks (also known as cinder block), but they are most often coated with a colored coat of stucco or concrete for landscaping purposes.

USE WALLS AS BACKDROPS. Border walls create a clear separation between the house and the landscape, making the landscape design more of a contained "package." The beds in this yard take full advantage of the walls, basically using them as backdrop to show off different plant shapes, forms, and colors. You can use plain flat walls in any garden to great effect in this way.

ADD BRIGHT, EYE-POPPING COLORS. Embolden your yard with poured and painted concrete walls. As the low wall here shows, you can use just about any color, although colors that mimic flowers or foliage in landscaping plantings are some of the most effective. The wall's crisp lines and hard surfaces contrast the surrounding plantings and, coupled with the color, make this as much an ornamental feature as a practical landscape structure. Because of the stability, you can use poured concrete walls on terraces, tall or short, and to hold back large sections of earth.

CONTROL THE CHAOS. Here, stacked flagstone walls create an informal and almost accidental look; the material matches the stepping stones and steps up a hill. The somewhat chaotic look meshes perfectly with the haphazard pattern of plantings and the generally wild look of this landscape.

CAP WALLS PROPERLY. Cap a stone wall with flat pieces of cut flagstone to create a finished look to an informal wall. This wall was dry laid with alternating layers that help create a strong structure. The top cap provides a wonderful place to put container plants or to use as additional seating. You can also mortar wide top caps onto brick walls and stacked fieldstone walls.

STANDALONE WALLS CREATE BORDERS. A curving ornamental wall is a highly visual divider perfect for setting off and bordering an outdoor living room. Walls such as these, with formal lines and well-defined shapes, clearly delineate different areas, especially in a landscape where you're including a distinctive outdoor room such as this patio-bound social area.

MAKE WALLS FOR THE AGES. Concrete can be an ideal material for building terraced hillside walls; it is easily reinforced and can be sized and shaped to suit the circumstance. It can also be finished in a number of different looks, including the whitewash shown here. This is an elegant design, with different shapes of walls, retaining tidy beds and steps leading up to a top ledge that showcases a tiered fountain. Use a design like this and you can choose to keep the plants neat and contained, or allow them to overgrow the beds and soften the look of the concrete surfaces.

Landscape Walls and Steps

USE WALLS AS TRANSITIONS. Successful landscape design has much to do with effective transitions, and stone walls are excellent devices to create fluid transitions within a yard. This fieldstone wall includes the obvious transition from one level to another, but also makes for a visually sensible change from a rough, irregular stepping stone path to the more regimented look of a brick path. Repetitive plantings help the transition make sense.

WALLS AND STEPS CAN ADD HIGH DRAMA. Stone walls and steps often seem so utilitarian and plain that it's easy to forget that they can make grand, dramatic statements in a landscape. The designer of this landscape had just that in mind, creating a semi-circular staircase out of stone, with a shape that is replicated throughout the landscape design. It's a stunning feature and one that—in contrast to the various plantings—will be an unchanging anchor to the look and style of the landscape for a very long time to come.

ONE STEP LEADS TO ANOTHER. A mix of materials and shades make these very interesting steps. Not only has the designer used four different hardscape materials for the pathway and steps, they are all set against a distinctive wood-sided house. The use of irregular slabs for the steps also contrasts the geometric style of the paver pathway.

USE TIMBERS TO TAME A SLOPE. Landscape steps in a steep slope are a feature that demands a certain precision and layout. The timbers used on this severe grade are ideal, because the wood absorbs changes within the soil and is less likely to shift out of position than stones or slabs. They are also cut to standardized measurements, so figuring out tread and riser measurements is easier than working with irregularly sized pieces. The one caveat in using timbers as walls or steps is to ensure they haven't been treated with toxic chemicals such as creosote, which might leach and pollute the soil or water table.

BUILD WITH LOCAL STONE. The walls here are mortared fieldstone from a nearby quarry. Although stacked walls look wonderful, when a landscape wall needs to buttress tons of dirt, it's wisest to use a reinforced mortared border to ensure that the wall lasts as long as the slope does.

ARRANGE STONE ARTISTICALLY. A stacked fieldstone wall can be a magical element in the landscape. The stone pops out against the expanse of an emerald lawn, providing a riveting textural switch from a smooth lawn, to the tumble of soft plants on the slope above. There is a natural visual progression upward, with different textures at every level.

COMBINE STEPS AND WALLS FOR A SMOOTH TRANSITION. Integrating a stone wall and steps into the landscape is much more seamless if the bed they border is tightly populated with masses of plants. A thick dense growth sprawling over the top edge of a wall, and brushing the borders of stone steps, is a sure way to make the design look mature and natural. It's as if the structure had been there from the time the house was built. This wall curves to embrace a small stone patio visitors cross in making their way to the front door.

CUT STONE AND RUBBLE STONE GO TOGETHER. Stone steps and walls are great places to mix materials and looks. The angled walls and steps in this front yard are an intriguing combination of mortared fieldstones topped with crisp, cut stone segments that provide sharp lines as counterpoints to the rounded irregular shapes below them. This is a great look for just about any style of landscape and provides the added bonus of a lot of extra seating along the top caps.

USE BROAD STEPS TO CONQUER A MILD SLOPE. Deep and wide steps like this are comfortable and safe passageways for visitors to climb a slope. The combination of textured concrete and rough-cut curbstone nosings is not only a spectacular look, but also a guide to the eye so that you'll unconsciously know exactly when to step—a feature that helps prevent the accidental trips that are common to deep steps like these. Combined, they create an ideal design that works well to traverse a long, mild slope in your landscape.

USE CRUSHED STONE FOR A VERY NATURAL LOOK. However, it's imperative to define the steps with solid nosings of some sort, such as the timbers used here. The nosings keep the stone on each level in place, help prevent erosion of the steps over time, and give visual cues where to rise. Nosings can be any of a number of materials, but they need to be sturdy to hold up over time and in the face of the elements.

Hardscaping with Decks and Patios

ISLAND DECKS HAVE EXOTIC APPEAL. Make a small deck a hidden stage for maximum impact from the structure. Slightly elevated, this landscape platform is nestled amidst a profusion of plant growth and backed by a painted garden wall. It hosts two chairs for relaxing and a sculptural outdoor light, creating a scene that is tranquil, artistic, and blends perfectly with the surroundings.

CLEAR RAILINGS TURN A PATIO INTO A BALCONY. Hardscape patio surfaces can stand in for traditional decks, providing solid, stable platforms in the landscape. This viewing and dining patio features a lovely arbor and a transparent railing on three sides and contributes to the pleasing overall aesthetic. The patio has been positioned at the edge of a small lawn to take advantage of the wild view down a wooded slope. Where there is a spectacular view, it's a good idea to position your hardscape, or deck, to take advantage of it.

EXPERIMENT WITH UNUSUAL MATERIALS. This ipé deck seems to meld into its naturalistic surroundings. The homeowner has run the mulched beds around the border under the actual deck, blurring boundaries. A mix of planted and potted plants reinforces the union between structure and landscape, with vegetation growing right up against the edges of the deck.

A LANDING CAN FUNCTION LIKE A PATIO. Here, a stone stairway with a spacious landing has been constructed with a modest waterfall and pond built into the side. Always look to exploit any area of the landscape to its maximum potential.

Hardscaping with Decks and Patios

BLEND WOOD AND STONE. Mix wood decking with hard patio surfaces to create intriguing contrasts. The wood complements the natural elements in the landscape and the lines of the deck reinforce the lines in the hardscape.

ADD A FLOCK OF FLOWERING BASKETS. A deck should be integrated into the landscape as seamlessly as possible, but you can still be just as creative with deck structures as you can with other landscape features. This unorthodox octagonal arbor offers a great focal point with lots of lines and attractive weathered wood, but the designer also took the opportunity to use the cross braces as support for a series of identical hanging baskets. It's a one-of-a-kind look that embellishes the whole landscape.

Hardscaping with Decks and Patios

WOOD DECKS INVITE GREENERY. Although a wood deck at ground level is easy to build and can truly integrate into the surrounding landscape, a slightly elevated structure provides a platform for dining, relaxing, or entertaining, with a vantage point over the entire landscape. For decks butted up against a building on one side, a little elevation can add to the deck and the landscape.

WOOD DECKS AND WATER FEATURES ARE ENCHANTING. This landscape incorporates an Asian design style in a small space with a large pond. The deck runs right up to the water's edge, creating a tropical feel, and providing an elegant dining area that is a stunning design accent wet or dry. Whenever you begin looking at hardscape options around a pool or pond, throw wood into the mix—it requires a little bit more work to construct a deck, but the results can be exceptional.

Hardscaping with Decks and Patios

REDEFINE DECKING. The mixed surface shown here, combining loose rock infill with embedded boards, is anything but traditional decking. It is, however, an ideal surface for an outdoor kitchen; the boards provide stable footing, while the loose stone provides a great deal of decorative appeal and a surface that conceals the inevitable spills that come with outdoor food prep and dining.

DEFINE SPACES BY FUNCTION. Combine decking and patios to create independent areas in the landscape. Decks are great ways to define particular areas, especially recreational areas such as the spa tub platform shown here. The decking itself blends with the naturalistic surroundings, but the construction sets the tub area apart from the rest of the yard and contains the function of the space very neatly.

LET DECKING TAKE A BACK SEAT IN DESIGN. Use a large, flat deck such as this in the same way you would a lawn or plain hardscaped surface—as a visual break between more dynamic landscape elements. One of the wonderful things about decks is that the deck structure itself can easily be designed around existing elements such as trees or ponds, integrating them into the deck and integrating the deck into the yard. This is also a low-maintenance alternative to a lawn and is easier to build than inlaid pavers.

Hardscapes and Water

USE CUT STONE TO FRAME A LOVELY PICTURE. Hardscape surfaces are highly effective for adding order to a landscape. That's no truer than with precisely cut pavers, such as the stones that make up the paths and patio in this yard. The hard, flat, clearly defined areas of stone stand in stark contrast to the flowing organic shapes of the pond area and the rest of the garden. This is essentially a way to "color within the lines" by establishing hardscape borders that guide the eye and provide visual relief from the busy grouping of plants.

FLAGSTONE MAKES FIRST-RATE POOL DECKING. Be creative with hardscaping around a pool to make both the pool and the surrounding area more attractive. An irregular stone surface such as this provides interesting visual contrast to the geometric shape of the pool, and the color of the flagstone variations adds variety to the alluring blue of the water. Natural, uncut stones go well with the surrounding seafront grasses and landscape, and a matching border wall supplies both a sitting area and clear separation between the pool and the landscaped side yard.

CREATE MARGINAL AREAS AROUND WATER FEATURES. Where a patio abuts a water feature, create a smooth transition for the best possible appearance. Here, the designer used a border of flowers with a small white fence to create separation from the hardscape and the pond. This provides a way for the eye to seamlessly glide from one surface to another without a jarring contrast. You could also make this transition with a row of low hedges, a strip of infill or soil, or a line of river rocks or boulders.

PROVIDE A STABLE ACCESS POINT. Create a stunning look on a slope leading down to a pond by installing a large rock "bank" from the pond upward. The designer here added stairs to help visitors navigate down to the edge of the pond, but small boulders arranged across the slope give this water feature a very naturalistic look. This effect works best on gentle slopes; on more severe inclines the rocks or boulders will have to be dug into the slope to keep them from rolling or sliding down toward the water.

ANTI-SKID SURFACES CAN BE ATTRACTIVE. Stone blocks make some of the most fascinating hardscape surfaces, especially around a pool. As this patio clearly shows, the pitted surfaces create an antique feel, as if it had been around for centuries. The surface also serves a practical purpose: it's never slick when wet, offering a safe floor for swimmers to get in and out of the pool. Choose stone slabs and tiles with an eye toward subtle color variations, as this design of this surface did.

BUILDERS HAVE ORGANIC IMPACT. Here, a low block wall borders a curving paver hardscape surface that wraps around an artificial pond. The wall follows the curve, giving it more of an organic shape, and doubles as a bench. But the boulders are the element that brings nature back.

Water Features

Water is one of the most enchanting elements you can add to a landscape design. We are fascinated by all things liquid, especially when the natural power and grace of nature can be harnessed for display in one's backyard. There's no reason not to consider adding streams, rivers, ponds, pools, and waterfalls to your landscape.

Integrating any of these into your landscape involves deciding on which best suits the design you're after. It's also a matter of how much effort and expense you're willing to expend. A static water feature, such as a basic birdbath or simple stone basin, is the easiest to incorporate. But the real magic is in larger features, and especially those that involve moving water. If you're not looking to plumb or run electricity, you can still install a lovely pond choosing from readily available liners and accessories. With just a little more effort and investment, you can incorporate a waterfall over a pool, a small flowing stream, or a recirculating birdbath.

Regardless of which you choose, a landscape water feature is great for inviting wildlife into the yard. Birds will flock to the clean water of a birdbath, and koi are a natural addition to a pond. Just be clear that where birds and fish reside, other animals—including neighborhood cats, raccoons, and deer—are sure to follow. You may need to add significant fencing or other barricades to protect your landscape. Local ordinances probably require fencing to keep neighborhood kids out as well.

MAKE THE WATER MOVE. Enrich a small yard by adding a tiny pond such as this one. It provides a wonderful centerpiece for a tranquil spot meant for unwinding from the day's pressures. The gazing ball fountain in this pond is equipped with a pump that provides the soft gurgling stream of water. The entire feature can be installed in a couple weekends by anyone with even moderate DIY skills.

WATERFALLS OFFER ENDLESS FASCINATION. If you have the space in your yard, a complete water course is an unparalleled landscape feature. This backyard features a naturalistic stream with cascading levels ending in a koi pond. When possible, construct your water feature for movement. The beauty of a water feature with flowing water is that it adds alluring sounds to the visual feast of your landscape. The burbling of the stream and splash of the waterfall make this scene even more inviting than it already was.

LOOK INTO LIVESTOCK. As captivating as a pond might be, it's even more so when stocked with koi. It's one way to make the pond look natural, rather than manmade. This pond was designed with a small waterfall, which conceals the filter and recirculating pump—all of which helps keep the waterborne environment healthy for the fish. Always make sure any pond you stock with koi is at least two feet deep, preferably with small niches or crannies; the idea is to help the fish avoid predators because large birds and other wildlife find koi a tasty snack.

Ponds

PONDS COME IN ALL SHAPES AND SIZES. Where the garden design is more formal and linear, the pond shape should follow those cues. This sophisticated backyard features cut stone, classic statuary, and linear structures such as arbors, so it only makes sense to design the water features to complement all the other elements of the design. A landscape pond is alluring in any shape, especially when it fits the rest of the landscape.

SITE YOUR POND IN SUNLIGHT. Ponds are most often used as accent features in a landscape with other areas of the same or greater design interest. However, that's not a law, and you shouldn't think of it as such. The designer of this brightly sunlit landscape opted to put the pond dead center in the middle of the lawn. It's unusual, but it works.

TAKE A WALK ON THE WATER SIDE. Pathways and ponds are like peanut butter and jelly: they work just fine as separate elements, but the combination is dynamite. There are a lot of ways to design a pathway in tandem with a pond. One of the most visually impressive—and just plain cool—is to mount stepping stones on secure pillars, running steps right across the water (top). If you're not willing to go to that much effort, or if your pond is too modest to merit a crossing pathway, you should still consider wrapping any path through the landscape around the pond (bottom). This is a way to give visitors to the yard and garden multiple points of view from which to enjoy the water. That's a great way to think about ponds but also about any other feature in the landscape. Always ask, "How will it look from other vantage points?"

Ponds

MARRY PONDS AND MARGINAL PLANTS. Ponds are natural choices for deep-shade areas of the garden where a bed or other plantings would have a hard time surviving, much less thriving. That's why it's usually best to select plants to fill in around the water feature by their ability to grow in shady, wet conditions. Foliage plants such as the hostas shown here are natural partners to a pond, as are the ferns growing by the pond. Fill in with the appropriate plants and you blend the pond perfectly, making it seem that much more like a natural feature of the landscape.

CREATE A BALANCED ECOSYSTEM. The richest parts of most any landscape are the living things; without growing flora, the landscape becomes just an exercise in outdoor decorating. Complement other plants in your landscape with life added to the pond. Koi are great additions to a pond, and can even tolerate cold winters as long as the pond doesn't freeze and there is a constant supply of oxygen and nutrients. Water plants such as the lily pads shown here actually help aerate the water and control algae blooms, creating not only a beautiful scene, but also a great environment for the fish.

COPING STONES HOLD POND LINERS BUT ALSO GUIDE YOUR EYE. A large pond requires a great deal of planning and work, but the reward is an amazing and one-of-a-kind landscape feature. One of the best ways to blend the pond into its surroundings—aside from the extensive plantings around this pond—is to line the borders of the pond with a mixture of small and large river rocks. It's a scene right out of the wilderness, and a captivating one at that.

Waterfalls

WATERFALLS PROVIDE MULTIPLE BENEFITS. A fast-moving waterfall efficiently aerates the water, helping create a healthier environment for the fish in the pond. But the more tangible benefit in terms of the landscape is a riveting water feature that is fascinating to watch and provides a white-noise background that's pleasing to the ears. A waterfall such as this requires only a pump, a few feet of tubing, and the rocks and soil to create the foundation. Take your time, because a poorly designed waterfall structure ruins the naturalistic illusion.

WATERFALLS CAN HELP MAKE PONDS SWIMMABLE. There are many ways to design a landscape waterfall, but one of the most popular is as a way to recirculate pool water through the filtration system. There are tons of options, but this is one of the most attractive. The landscaper has used stacked fieldstone with water lines routed from the filter, running water down the rock faces and back into the pool. It's a great way to combine the natural allure of a rock-face waterfall, with the compelling luxury of a swimming pool.

WATER FEATURES CAN HAVE TINY FOOTPRINTS. No room to install a full-scale water feature? No worries; you can capture much of the magic of moving water with a small-scale feature such as this. You won't find a more dynamic landscape accent than a well-thought-out mound of rocks with a tiny waterfall splashing into a miniature pool. This design could fit into any corner of the yard, and can actually be run off a solar-powered pump, eliminating the need for wiring to the location.

CREATE YOUR OWN BLUE LAGOON. A pond is the perfect addition to a tropical landscape theme, especially where sun is abundant and the climate is generally warm. This particular pond is surrounded by tropical plant species and features a "trickle" waterfall that creates quite a different sound than rushing water. It's an interesting variation on the usual fast-moving waterfall, and the entire scene suggests "vacation." Landscape around the pond to suit the theme of the yard—and enrich it.

Waterfalls

USE A WATER FEATURE AS AN ACCENT. Waterfalls don't have to be connected to a pond or any other water feature, as this patio scene clearly shows. The dining area is set up to take advantage of the scintillating view of a waterfall spouting forth from a mortared wall. This is a great way to have a stunning water feature where there isn't room or the appropriate situation for a full-blown pond.

GET ECLECTIC WITH WATER. Here, a series of stepped urns creates a lightly flowing waterfall that recirculates endlessly. Although the artfully arranged urn pitchers may look like a designed composition, this is actually a single unit sold with pump and pedestal as a place-anywhere waterfall for the landscape. All you need is an outdoor outlet and you can have your own miniature waterfall accent trickling away in a matter of minutes.

CREATE AN ALPINE ENVIRONMENT. The designer of this waterfall incorporated a sprawling groundcover variety of the juniper shrub. It's a tough plant, able to thrive in many different soil types, including the rocky formation here. But, just as importantly, its growth habit is put to perfect sculptural use, draping along the form of the waterfall rocks as if the shrubs were liquid. Keep shrub shapes in mind when planning them into your design.

CREATE A WATERY SURPRISE. A waterfall can be the perfect way to liven up otherwise ordinary stone walls. Installed in the middle of the wall, with a modest return basin underneath, the waterfall is an unexpected element that seems to work perfectly against the natural stone surfaces and alongside plantings of shade-loving foliage species. Look for unexpected places to put your own waterfall to bring a surprising element to some otherwise low-key corner of your landscape.

Pools

LANDSCAPING MAKES A POOL IMPROVEMENT.
A plain, undistinguished pool just needed some landscape "sprucing up" to come to life. A new seating pavilion structure creates a wonderful social center at one end of the pool, while a row of white-foliaged, shade-loving plants provides a burst of brightness along the fence. Simple additions, but sometimes that's all it takes to make the area around a pool more inviting and more special.

IRREGULAR POOL SHAPES LOOK MORE NATURAL.
A rambling landscape works best around an irregularly shaped pool. As this example shows, an odd shape will echo some of the natural forms and outlines in the rest of the landscape, blending in well with the natural surroundings. Wrap dense plantings around one or more edges of the pool to amplify the effect and blend the pool even more seamlessly into the surrounding landscape design.

LOOK INTO AN INFINITY EDGE. "Zero horizon" pools—also commonly called "infinity edge"—are a fascinating style that can be a perfect choice for any side of the landscape with a transition or drop-off ledge. Here, the vanishing edge disappears into a desert that the property borders. The shimmering water and the desert scene create a stunning contrast that the edge of the pool emphasizes. Infinity edge pools can't be used everywhere, but where they can, it's a great way create an incredible visual.

POOLS CAN BE ORNAMENTAL, TOO. This small, tiled wading pool was scaled down to fit the constrained proportions of the yard, but it still provides big visual bang. The elevated sides of the pool create an elegant surround with white concrete caps that double as extra seating. The pool water is filtered through a slit waterfall perfectly suited to the overall elegance of the water feature. If you are not ready for a full-size swimming pool, or if your budget or yard size simply isn't big enough to handle one, a smaller wading pool such as this can be a compromise without sacrifice.

GO TROPICAL REGARDLESS OF CLIMATE. Tropical plantings are a natural landscape element around any pool. As this landscape shows, palm trees and hot-weather blooming plants present a lush backdrop to the inviting blue water. As long as you live in a fairly warm climate, you can create an environment of varied shapes, textures, and shades of green to enjoy while sunbathing or swimming. Many of these plants do surprisingly well even in states with cold winter temperatures. Pick carefully, and you can create your own Caribbean getaway in the backyard.

SURROUND YOUR POOL WITH A LOVELY LANDSCAPE. Dress up your bare-bones swimming pool with a fun themed look. The right approach can bring a big dash of whimsy to the landscape at large while making the pool area that much more enjoyable to use. Here, the homeowner has created a beach look, with bright umbrellas scattered around the pool, and an outdoor bar set on a crescent of sand. It's vacation-style landscaping that the homeowners can use every day of the week.

MAKE THE POOL THE FOCAL POINT. A neat, trim black fence (as much for safety as for style) surrounds this standard, rectangular pool, creating a uniform look even before the plantings were considered. The look is restrained by surrounding the pool by a border of lawn, edged at the fence with a scattering of low-maintenance evergreens. It's a subtle and subdued design. It's also neat and reads visually "clean"—if your pool is generally full of children and partying visitors, it might pay to introduce a less complex landscape such as this.

LANDSCAPE LIGHTS CAN BE PERFECT FOR POOLS. Swimming pools at night are almost always enchanting visions, but the question is always how to light around them. Here, the designer has answered that question by letting the swimming pool interior lights—and a ring of romantic candles—supply all the illumination for the yard. A privacy screen of tall evergreen shrubs on one side creates a visual block, preventing the view from a neighboring house. The opposite side is lined with low ornamental grasses, leaving the dark vista as a mysterious view and the perfect stargazing opportunity. It's wise to consider the night view when landscaping around a pool.

Wall Fountains

ADD A BEAUTIFUL BASIN. A wall fountain is an intriguing decorative element and can be made even more so by a creative choice of vessel to receive the water that comes out of the fountain. For instance, this sculptural wall fountain adorns an ivy covered brick wall—all part of a captivating visual. But the blue urn set on a bed of river rocks enhances the look and adds a unique element to what is already a unique water feature. If you go to the trouble of installing a spout for a wall-mounted fountain, consider less obvious options as basins for the water flow.

MYTHOLOGICAL FORMS ARE FULL OF FANCY. Go traditional with your wall fountain by using a lion's head spout. These have been used for centuries and still serve as an engaging visual. You can find simple lion's head spouts that are meant to be attached to an existing wall, without any surrounding structure. It's a good option for a low-key and simple wall fountain.

FISH MAKE NATURAL FOUNTAIN FORMS. Wall-mounted fountains make wonderful surprises in the garden. Positioned among a tumble of foliage on a brick wall, this handsome fountain is a common style, with a figural image used as a spout (in this case, a fish) and a basin beneath to catch the water. Other styles spout the water directly into a small pond or pool in the ground. Wall fountains tend to look best when surrounded by growth, as if they were an old mortared fixture that just happened to be part of the wall.

THE GREEK GOD PAN SHOWS UP FREQUENTLY IN FOUNTAINS. Wall-mounted "face" fountains are a traditional garden addition throughout europe, and one that strikes a chord with many landscape designers in this country. As this example shows, the sculpture spout looks like a face, creating not only an eye-catching water feature, but also a great ornament even when the water is off. Fountains such as this are often plumbed right through the wall, and powered only by water pressure; the trough basin simply drains the water.

STANDALONE FOUNTAINS LOOK LIKE WALL UNITS— BUT WITH NO INSTALLATION REQUIRED. It is extremely difficult to mount a unit on the framed wall of the house (wall-mounted fountains are most commonly mounted on tall garden walls), so this solution is ideal. Although the plantings around the fountain are immature, it's clear to see the design intention was for plants to eventually cloak the fountain and visually reinforce the idea of a surface-mounted feature. It's an interesting and useful technique you can use to integrate many different types of landscape features and ornaments.

Free-standing Fountains

SELF-CONTAINED FOUNTAINS ARE "PLUG-AND-PLAY." Fountains come in all shapes and sizes, including this black pillar in the style of carved stone. When you consider unusual fountains for your landscape, you open up your options in terms of form and color. As this fountain shows, you can opt for an ebony glaze that seems wet almost all the time. Most styles such as this are simply plugged into an outdoor outlet or power source—the pump and plumbing are inside. The self-contained design makes positioning and repositioning the fountain a much easier task.

ORANTE FOUNTAINS ARE THE FOCAL POINT IN SOME DESIGN TRADITIONS. Here, a large and spectacular terra cotta-colored fountain sits on its own square courtyard. The courtyard is paved with crushed red stone, which carries through the strong color of the fountain. The Mexican and Southwest inspiration for the fountain is maintained in the blue glazed posts at each corner, supporting potted plants, as well as the neat geometric border (which contrasts the curves of the fountain) that contains series of cacti. It's an impressive and stylistically definitive approach.

THE PINEAPPLE DESIGN IS A CLASSIC. Positioned on a semicircle bump-out in a narrow patio, the fountain is ready to be activated. Choose a tiered fountain if you want a more pronounced splashing sound and are looking for a more vertical element of design. This fountain rises tall and the water pours over the lip of each basin into the next, creating both a lovely sound and nice visual. There's a reason why classic designs become classic.

DON'T TAKE FOUNTAINS LIGHTLY. A large fountain such as this requires a significant commitment because of its price and weighs over 500 pounds. However, its timeless cast-stone design brings big flair to any landscape style. If you're looking for an impressive centerpiece for a courtyard or even a lawn or large, flat bed, you could do far worse than making this investment. This particular fountain comes ready-to-assemble in four pieces, with integral motor and plumbing; just fill with water, plug it in, and enjoy.

Free-standing Fountains

USE A FOUNTAIN IN CONJUNCTION WITH A PERMANENT WATER FEATURE. A freestanding fountain doesn't necessarily mean freestanding on solid ground. This fountain is partially submerged and helps aerate the pond, just as a waterfall does. The spouting action can be adjusted to the height and volume that works best for your visual sense. It's a fountain worth considering if you have a pond to which you want to add a little zest.

USE FOUNTAINS FOR CUSTOM EFFECTS. This unique structure is a fountain, sculptural element, and pool all in one. Custom-made, it adds color, mesmerizing sound, and a curving organic shape to a corner of the landscape. If what you find at retail doesn't thrill you, keep in mind that you can always design your own fountain, even if it turns out to be something more than a fountain.

MAKE A DRIFTWOOD FOUNTAIN. This fountain is formed from a nozzle positioned inside a sculptural piece of driftwood that has been colored over time by exposure to the elements. It creates a more active and dynamic visual than most garden fountains. The nozzle pressure is adjustable, allowing the homeowner to change the presentation at a whim.

RETURN TO THE CLASSICS. This unorthodox fountain is shaped like a Grecian urn, an attractive and curvaceous form that complements the overgrown landscape. It has also been nestled in an out-of-the-way alcove, which lends mystery to the landscape. Depending on where you stand, the fountain may be heard but not seen. Hidden details like this, which reveal themselves only at certain vantage points in the yard, can be truly unique features of a well-thought landscape design.

FREESTANDING FOUNTAINS CAN BE MOVED FOR VARIETY OR IMPACT. Positioning a fountain in a square of vegetation, or even a different paving material than the rest of the patio, sets it apart and helps reinforce the idea that it is a special landscape element. The square of groundcover plants sprawling around this fountain's base gives the impression that there isn't a clear line where the fountain starts and the plants end. It's an organic look that can be used at the base of any structure and freestanding element in the garden.

Birdbaths

PUT YOUR BIRDBATH ON A PEDESTAL. Using a birdbath in this way—as the centerpiece of a very organized and designed planting—is making use of not only its functional purpose, but the elegant shape that serves here as ornament. This is an unusual but successful design, with the rigid lines of the walkway and bed contrasting the organic shapes of the plants and the curves of the birdbath. It's creative thinking—actually inside the box.

ANY VESSEL THAT HOLDS WATER WILL DO. This is perhaps the most basic style imaginable—a simple granite bowl that is placed on the ground. It's an engaging addition to the garden, but as a true birdbath, it needs to be positioned correctly. Birds like to sun themselves after bathing, so this should receive direct sun for a good part of the day. They also like clean water, so plan on changing the water in the basin frequently.

A GOOD BIRDBATH HAS ROUGH EDGES FOR REACHING. A white cement birdbath is a traditional design for gardens of all shapes and sizes. This style is usually fairly inexpensive, but durable, and the material fits right in as this one does, among dense foliage and landscape plants. This healthy habitat will make the birds feel right at home as they bathe. It's a visually pleasing placement that's sure to draw birds. If you have a cat in your house or neighborhood who regularly visits the garden, though, position a birdbath in the clear, so that birds can easily detect the movement of a tabby on the prowl.

Special Features

The many landscape design features available, such as trellises, arbors, or sculptures, are your key to embellishing your landscape and putting your personal stamp on the design. There is such an amazing variety of these features that you really should have no problem finding one or more that suits your design goals and available space perfectly.

They range from small to large, even within a given type. For instance, you can use a miniature pagoda statue as a modest accent to your Zen garden design, or spend a lot more on a life-size Buddha statue that will serve as an amazing focal point.

Start your search with the pragmatic. If your design needs a gate, a gate in a trellised archway adds a lot of visual power to what might otherwise be a simple portal. Climbing plants need something to climb, so a trellis becomes a necessity as well as a decorative element. Benches can add style while filling a need for extra seating. Statuary, gazing balls, sundials, and archways contribute to a landscape design as well, even if they don't serve a specific function.

In any case, always think about the purpose of what you're adding to the landscape. It doesn't need to be pragmatic, but every landscape design feature should have a design purpose: framing a view, accenting a planting, or complementing another feature.

Another decision you'll make in choosing landscape features is whether to build or buy. Because there are so many options at retail, the more common practice by far is to buy premade or "ready-to-assemble" features. Some features, such as cast-stone sundials or large statuary, will be beyond a homeowner's means to create. Others may be perfect do-it-yourself projects.

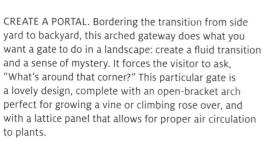

CREATE A PORTAL. Bordering the transition from side yard to backyard, this arched gateway does what you want a gate to do in a landscape: create a fluid transition and a sense of mystery. It forces the visitor to ask, "What's around that corner?" This particular gate is a lovely design, complete with an open-bracket arch perfect for growing a vine or climbing rose over, and with a lattice panel that allows for proper air circulation to plants.

BUY A MAINTENANCE-FREE ARCHWAY UNIT. This archway is sold as a complete unit, ready to assemble and place in your landscape. Take pains to mesh a pre-manufactured piece like this into the landscape. The designer of this yard scene has trained roses over and through the lattice construction, making the archway seem like a long-time member of a lush, beautiful garden scene. The arch is also placed on the first level of a series of deep steps, making it part of a natural transition between levels. Never place design features haphazardly—their positioning should reflect the same amount of thought you would put into a garden bed.

ADD A GREAT GATE. Gates, especially tall gates, can add to the sense of mystery in a landscape. This stylish gate features elegant woodworking details and an aged gray patina that makes it a focal point. The path leading to it and its solid form make the viewer naturally wonder what's on the other side. The matching enclosure for the central air-conditioning unit is a lovely touch, and one that makes a beautiful accent out of an otherwise unattractive yard element.

The ideas pictured here are a start. Although a bathtub used as a planter may be considered a bit low-brow, you can incorporate unusual repurposed or found objects in the landscape. You can also make your own original creations, or modify what you find at retail. Just be careful that you aren't "trashing up" the design. The lines, textures, and style of whatever you include should always complement the plantings and theme you've chosen for your landscape and be inherently attractive itself.

Arbors, Gates, and Arches

INTRODUCE SOME IRON. Steel can be an unusual look for a garden gate, and oval archway gates are a distinctive look in any landscape. This simple gate is meant as a decorative passageway, and the oval frames the focal point of the landscape: a three-tiered fountain. The strong black lines of the gate provide interesting contrast to its surroundings and clearly delineates the fountain from the pathway that runs by it. You can highlight features in your landscape this way to great effect.

OVERHEAD FEATURES HAVE A COZY EFFECT. Pergolas are great for defining landscapes and softening the edge between home and garden.

OVERHEAD STRUCTURES ARE MADE FOR TRAINING. Wrapped in fragrant roses, the formal backdrop of a pergola makes for a romantic summer setting and helps the transition from the patio to the yard.

ARCHWAYS ARE ALL ABOUT ROMANCE. Fine detailing sets exquisite garden features apart from the mundane. This spectacular bench and arbor unit features column caps, a Chippendale woodwork pattern in the bench back, and perfect proportions and lines. It's a lovely landscape retreat but also a stunning example of the type of well-designed features available for home landscapes. You'll find stylish units like this available in composite materials that are resistant to rot, insect infestation, and that don't need periodic maintenance such as repainting.

USE OVERHEAD STRUCTURES TO CREATE INTIMATE SPOTS. A large structure such as this double-bench pergola arbor deserves to be designed right into the landscape. The designer in this case set the unit in place as a passageway in the middle of a wall of shrubs. The brick footing and hanging baskets lend a sense of permanence and make this rustic sitting structure an area all its own. Use small touches like paved foundations to make a large-built feature seem like it's been a part of the landscape forever.

USE AN ARBOR TO COVER A WALKWAY. A large arbor creates its own separate area within the landscape. The arbor here provides broken, dappled shade over a brick paved patio. This purpose is hardly the only use a sizeable structure like this fills; arbors are natural supports for vigorous climbing vines and look beautiful cloaked in a sprawling green shawl. You can build an arbor—even a large one—much easier than most other landscape structures because the basic design is formed of straight lines and can easily be built with standard lumber sizes.

WELCOME VISITORS WITH A LOVELY PERGOLA. Pergolas are natural companions to garden gates. They form a more complete entryway into a given section of the landscape and add solidity, visual weight, and design flair to what is essentially a pretty simple opening in a fence. The structure here has been designed to appear as all of a piece; the lines in the pergola complement the lines in the gate, and the entire structure has been painted a clean, sharp white. It's a technique you can put to good use whenever you add a structure to another structure in your landscape.

MAKE A CUSTOM ENTRY THAT'S TRULY IMPRESSIVE. When you're willing to go the extra mile in terms of expense—or if you have experience in finish carpentry and a full woodworking shop—you can design custom entryways for your landscape. A spectacular entry such as this hardwood gate and gabled arbor befits a large, well-designed landscape. If you've put a lot of time and energy into creating a detailed multi-level landscape design with complex water features, statuary, and other high-end decorative features, a show-stopping entrance such as this gate might be the perfectly fitting introduction.

Arbors, Gates, and Arches

THE ROSE ARBOR IS A LANDSCAPING CLASSIC. You don't have to go to great extremes or great expense to have a truly memorable garden structure. A very basic trellis arbor like the one shown here can be stunning when coupled with the right flowering vine. The gray wood of this particular structure is handsome whether covered in flora or not, and the light weight means that it's portable—a handy feature when you want to change around the landscape design.

FRAME A DOORWAY WITH FLOWERING VINES. These vines fill this entryway with dappled light and fragrant air to be enjoyed with each pass through.

BUILD STRUCTURES IN SERIES. This is a creative interpretation of the arbor concept: using a series of arches, the builder has created an arbor-like tunnel that leads visitors through a closed entryway wreathed in beautiful clematis vines. This unique structure relies on overgrowth for most of its decorative and visual power. It would be far less stunning bare. If you use this idea, be aware that it works best crossing an otherwise empty space such as the lawn here.

THE WIDE WORLD OF WOOD ▶

Redwood with clear finish

Cedar with transparent stain

Treated pine with semi-transparent stain

Rough color with solid-body stain

Treated pine with paint

You can choose from a variety of finishes for your wood structure. A given finish will look different depending on the type of underlying wood. Paint, however, looks much the same on any wood, and the surface should be primed with an outdoor wood primer prior to painting. It's not always a great idea to paint, though, if the wood itself has a captivating color and grain pattern.

Cedar   Redwood   Pressure-treated pine

These three woods are used to construct the vast majority of wooden landscape structures. Although their natural appearance is different wood to wood, they all share a resistance to rot and insect damage, and all are durable and easy to work with. Pressure-treated wood, however, requires special fasteners to avoid corrosion and staining.

Gazebos and Pavilions

CREATE A RUSTIC RETREAT. A gazebo should be scaled to the yard and landscape. This modest little structure fits perfectly in the yard, and was simple to build. It uses railings that can purchased in sections, a simple foundation and deck, and very little ornamentation. Sometimes plainer is better; never lose sight that as much as gazebos are visual treats, the key benefit is a place to sit out of the sun, with a panoramic view of your well-designed landscape.

FIT YOUR GAZEBO IN A VISUAL FRAME. Gazebos can be grand structures without requiring the skills of a seasoned DIYer. This lovely vine-wrapped structure was built according to a relatively simple plan, and features basic baluster rails, square posts, and a linear header design. The most complex part of it was the roof, which was still fairly basic by do-it-yourself standards. Instead of being wired, the gazebo features lovely hanging candle lamps. Chances are you could build a structure like this; if you do, be sure and plant around it to give it the lush, verdant background that this beautiful structure enjoys.

MAKE AN OUTPOST WITH A PAVILION. A pavilion can be built on flat ground, on a patio, or mounted on a deck, as this one is. The design is somewhat simpler and less ornate than a gazebo, but the purpose is largely the same: provide shade, plenty of airflow, and allow for a 360-degree view of the landscape. Pavilions are generally easier to build because there are fewer angles than in a gazebo, and they are consequently better suited to less formal or less historical landscape themes. You can easily scale down a structure like this for a shaded seating space anywhere in your landscape.

IMPRESS WITH A FULL-SIZE FIREPLACE. It's okay to center landscaping around something other than a planting. This highly social area features a large brick patio perfect for family meals, sunbathing, and huge parties. But the gigantic stone fireplace dominates the design. An inviting feature on chilly nights (or any night for that matter), the fireplace structure is simply an impressive visual no matter how you look at it.

FIRE PITS ADD FUN AND FUNCTION. This backyard corner was neglected and largely unused space before the designer reorganized it. Adding hardscaping in the form of a patio, path, and stone border defined the different areas of use, and a built-in fire pit adds a nice welcoming feature to the patio. The fire pit includes a wide stone lip to hold beverages and food, making the area even more usable. Adding a modest fire pit like this to a stone patio is a fairly simple matter—and something worth considering if you're putting in a brand-new outdoor surface.

DRY-STACKED FIRE RINGS CAN BE USED AND MOVED. A stacked stone fire pit was designed into this paver patio amid intersecting hardscape textures. The design makes the fire pit the center of attention, but it's supported by irregular beds that cut into the hard lines of the patio and work with the shape of the fire pit to break up the formal geometric appearance. Where you have the room, it makes sense to create a relaxing social area around a fire pit, rather than tacking it onto an existing area.

OUTDOOR FIREPLACES CAN MATCH ANY DÉCOR. A built-in fireplace is not only an impressive standalone feature, it is also an excellent addition to emphasize certain distinctive styles. This white stucco fireplace built on the side of an octagonal-paver patio is perfectly in keeping with the Mediterranean motif. Vines trained up the face of the fireplace add a sense of age and integration into the garden, and the scene as a whole is inviting, charming, and exceptionally attractive.

Rock Gardens

A SIMPLE GROUPING IS EFFECTIVE. A collection of boulders serves as a sculptural element that provides mass to the landscape, playing rounded irregular shapes and hefty visual weight off of lighter and more changeable garden elements. A boulder grouping like this is a lovely element set against shrubs or in the middle of a bed of groundcover plants, or as it is used here, placed in the negative space of a lawn, next to a tree.

USE ROCKS AS ENTRY MARKERS. One or two specimen rocks can be set at the start of a walkway or drive to mark it for all to see. In colder climates these rocks also create landmarks for shoveling.

SET ROCKS INTO A SLOPE. Mounds and slopes are natural sites for boulders in the landscape because the site mimics where boulders will be found in the wild. The key is to position the boulder so that it is sunk into the incline—if it just rests on the surface, it looks visually unstable, as if it will roll down the slope—and out of place. When using boulders in this way, it's always better to conceal too much of the boulder than too little. Live with the look for some time, and then remove dirt as necessary to make the boulder more of an apparent design element.

TURN ROCK INTO LIVING ROCK. It's easy to get sculptural with boulders and stones, and one of the most compelling ways to do that is to create a garden mound such as the one shown here. This is a unique design that uses flat, rough-cut flagstone to separate the borders and create visual layers in the mound. It's not a composition you'll find in nature, but it looks very natural. This is a decorative element that works best in an informal landscape with lush growth so that the soft shapes and textures of the vegetation serve as counterpoint to the rock formation.

Sculptures
and Ornaments

THREE'S A CROWD. Stagger urns and pottery for visual interest. Urns and other vessels have long been used for decoration in landscapes small and large. The sensuous shapes and organic forms blend naturally with their surroundings, and they look good amidst plant growth or on hardscape surfaces. They also come with many different surface styles, including crafted textural treatments such as the swirls on these urns. Although these are new units, the finish gives the impression that they are antique, and the look brings old-country charm to the landscape.

LARGER URNS ARE USEFUL DESIGN ELEMENTS. Large sturdy urns are great accents for patios and hardscape sitting areas. Like the urns on this patio, the form provides a vertical element in contrast to the flat surface, and the rounded shape is a complement to nearly all the forms in the garden. It's a wonderful decorative element with the added bonus that it can be moved as desired. Use elements such as this as they are here— multiples used repetitively, which create design continuity over the span of a hardscaped surface, or throughout the landscape.

SCULPTURE ADDS PLAYFULNESS TO YOUR LANDSCAPE. The beauty of using small sculptures is that you can easily play around with composition and positioning. In this low-water landscape, a Buddha statue sits naturally under a tree and seems to be grinning at the witty metal statuette that offers a much more modern style. It's a fun look, one that plays with obvious contrasts, and that can be quickly and easily changed to suit the homeowner's whim.

EVERY YARD SHOULD HAVE A FEW ROUND FORMS. Some of the best sculptural forms in a landscape are the simplest. Three orbs of varying sizes form a compelling grouping in this corner of a tropical landscape. Several visual dynamics and principles are at work here: the rounded forms of the spheres contrast the spiky forms of the palms; the odd number of spheres is much more intriguing than an even number of objects would have been. The variations in size adds visual interest, and the difference in colors and surface sheen makes sure the balls read against the background—if they had all been the same rough, natural texture, they might have visually fallen back into the textures behind them.

ADD SCULPTURES AND ORNAMENTS TO SHOWCASE CREATIVITY. A bit of wit often distinguishes a landscape decoration. Here, a fish finial tops a wavy lantern post, turning a functional fixture into decorative flair. The fish points the way on the journey along a garden path, and the post seems almost cartoonish. Always keep in mind that landscape ornaments can be your chance to have a little bit of fun. You can always remove them if they don't live up to the billing.

Sculptures and Ornaments

A SUNDIAL WILL NEVER GO OUT OF STYLE. Sundials are classic garden ornaments and come in many different styles. The blocky square post of this particular sundial gives it a solid, weighty look that works perfectly with the flowing spread of flowering annuals at its base. Sundials usually look best when placed among low-growing plants, rather than positioned on a hardscape surface. The exception to this general rule is a very ornate or antique sundial that deserves to be seen up close. In that case, it makes sense to provide a pad underneath as a display stage.

A LITTLE WHIMSY GOES A LONG WAY. Even small figures such as this one create a lot of visual interest as surprising elements nestled in a bed or breaking up a border comprised of multiples of the same plant. Unlike large "focal point" sculptures, small ones need to be positioned exactly where they'll bring the most bang for the buck. Experiment with your modest sculpture to make sure it is viewable from many different vantage points but that it is also nestled alluringly among plant growth.

USE GARDEN ORNAMENTS THAT PLAY WITH LIGHT. Gazing balls are aptly named because the color and reflective coating make this garden ornament mesmerizing. They are often placed on posts, although this gazing ball has been set on a low platform, nestled among a variety of foliage and flowers. The brilliant color and alluring shape make this look like a jewel placed into an organic setting, even more of a standout for its surroundings. The trick to getting the most out of a gazing ball is to use its reflective nature to best advantage, as has been done here.

A DISTINCT ELEMENT ADDS INTEREST TO A WATER FEATURE. Gazing balls are normally set in the garden on display among flowers. But doing the unexpected often leads to enchanting results in a landscape; and putting a gazing ball in a pond is certainly unexpected. The look is magical though. The water reflects back the image of the ball, and the ball reflects the image of the water. It's like a colored bubble floating on the surface of the water, and it's a look that works perfectly. You could just as easily marry a gazing ball to a small reflecting pool, the top or bottom of a waterfall, or among the rivulets in a stream.

Landscape Boundaries

On rare occasions, leaving the borders of your landscape open to a broad vista might be ideal; most landscapes, however, need a visual and physical stopping point. Although this is most often a fence of some kind, that's not a rule. The boundaries of your landscape can be defined by walls, or by living structures such as a row of tightly grouped shrubs or espaliered trees.

Given these options, the first decision to make is whether you want the boundary to be an unimposing backdrop, or a dynamic visual itself. Borders, living or not, are integral parts of a landscape design. You need to decide how vivid that part should be.

You'll also need to take into account practical considerations. Landscape boundaries aren't just visual. If you live in a semi-rural area surrounded by wildlife, you may need a very tall, solid fence to prevent animals such as deer from invading the yard and stripping the planted parts of your landscape. A smaller fence may suffice to keep neighborhood dogs out of your yard. The height of the border will also be determined by how much privacy you want in your landscape and how tall adjacent buildings are.

A living border can, of course, be stunning, but keep in mind that any plant you might use for a boundary line structure will take time to grow. You may want to spend a bit more money and buy mature plants so that you can have the living wall you need immediately.

Whatever you choose as the border of your landscape, keep the overall design in mind. Although a simple wood board fence might be an inoffensive backdrop, a detailed structure might actually complement a formal design more effectively, or use a rough log fence for your wild garden. Even as you look to contain your landscape design, never miss an opportunity to embellish it.

A HIGH-END FENCE MAKES A DRAMATIC DESIGN STATEMENT. Any fence has the potential to be part of the showcase look of your landscape design. Lattice-top wood fences are some of the most popular because they work with many different landscaping styles and present a handsome appearance. A fence like this can also be a fairly easy do-it-yourself project; this fence was constructed from pre-fab panels. Accurately set the posts, and building the fence is a simple process.

Before

After

MAKE A FENCE A FOCAL POINT. The side yard landscape of this seaside home had become unruly and disorganized—a neglected section of an otherwise stunning yard. The new landscape design includes rearranging shrubs and laying out the space with a small lawn, a pathway through to the swimming pool in the back, and a high-style fence that defines the entire space. The wood fence is a custom design combining lattice panels and open gridwork, and includes a spectacular arched gate through which the water can be seen. If you can afford a custom fence like this, the design can add immeasurably to the look and organization of the landscape.

YOU CAN'T GO WRONG WITH A PICKET FENCE. The iconic white picket fence remains as popular as ever. That's because it's a pleasing look, with a graphic rhythm that is the visual equivalent to the sound of train wheels. A fence such as this is not only easy to build, it sets a quaint and pretty tone for the landscape design. It also provides a starting point for the eye, setting up the design elements to come. A picket fence is not right for every home—it would look odd with a modern or Southwestern house—but it does work with many homes and landscapes, and is a classic look.

COMBINE FENCE STYLES. Fences can be used to define boundaries other than around the perimeter of a landscape. This fence creates a crisp demarcation between a wide path leading to the front door, and the landscape proper. The separation is made more blatant by the fact that the fence has been painted white to match the path's loose infill. This particular fence combines the heft of a rail fence with the lightness of pickets.

DON'T SACRIFICE PRIVACY AT THE EXPENSE OF STYLE. Here, the variety of plants in an island bed pops out toward the viewer against a simple thin-board, closed-design fence in the background.

USE PLANTINGS TO SOFTEN HARD-SURFACE FENCING. Iron fencing looks unique in any yard, but it can also be a bit severe. It often helps to soften the look as has been done here, with a variety of plants trained up and growing through the iron bars and crosspieces. It combines the utility of a fence and the loveliness of a trellis. The fence allows for air and light to reach the plants and the plants help block a bit of the view through the bars. It's a great strategy to make an iron fence seem a little more a part of the landscape design.

BUILD A LATTICE FENCE FOR VICTORIAN STYLING. Lattice-panel fences are popular for very good reasons. Not only is the look attractive, the panels allow for airflow and sunlight penetration to keep plants healthy, and they are perfect surfaces on which to train climbing plants or clinging vines. The white style shown here provides a clean, fresh appeal to the boundaries of a landscape design. Arched gateways are perfect partners to a stretch of lattice fence. You'll find that this type of fence is also fairly easy to install.

EXPERIMENT WITH EXOTIC MATERIALS. Bamboo is an exceptional material because it's strong and lightweight, easy to work with, and looks like nothing else. The two fences here represent two different styles. Create a more constrained look by simply framing the bamboo within the same rail and brace system you would use in a board fence (top). This fence used pressure treated wood for a durable low-key appearance that could serve as a background in most any garden style. The fence below is framed in segments outlined by redwood members, which creates a more distinctive, more Asian-influenced style. The look is perfectly suited to a design marked by bamboo plantings, ornamental grasses, and a copper-and-black obelisk fountain on top of a river rock base.

FENCES ARE REQUIRED FOR POOLS, BUT THEY ARE ALSO RESTRICTED IN HEIGHT AND SETBACK. Closed-fence designs are perfect for certain landscapes, such as a pool scene. Border plantings are a natural companion to the solid visual surface, but be sure you know how the design will affect sun exposure. As this image shows, a solid fence casts a pure shadow. Always know where the fence will create shadow so that you don't position full-sun plants in those areas.

FEW FENCES ARE AS REFINED AS WROUGHT IRON. A finely detailed wrought iron fence deserves to be shown off. This elegance befits a formal garden, although the fence will work with many other styles as well—from a cottage garden to a Southern style. On a practical note, you couldn't find a stronger fence. The half-height fence shown here is the most common style for wrought iron fences with this level of craftsmanship. However, a taller wrought iron fence could be an imposing element in a formal landscape.

Fences

FENCES MAKE FINE BACKDROPS FOR FLOWERS. The material and construction of a fence can add a captivating look to the landscape. In this case, a vertical shiplapped construction and cedar lumber give this fence an interesting appearance, without it being overly designed. However, no matter what construction is used to build a tall fence, it is almost always improved with base plantings that blur the seam between the bottom of the fence and the ground. Bushy foliage and flowering plants create a very natural and beautiful transition from the horizontal plane of the ground to the vertical surface of the fence.

A FENCE CAN BE A CANVAS. Positioned behind a small pavilion and a moderate-sized swimming pool, this solid board fence is meant as a privacy screen. Fences around pools often only need to block the view from neighbors' yards, because the pool area itself offers abundant visual interest. This fence is used for a display surface as well, with mounted decorative panels lining the section behind the pavilion.

PERSONALIZE YOUR FENCE WITH AN INDIVIDUAL FLOURISH. You don't need fancy construction to add a bit of flair to a very basic privacy fence. This board fence is about as basic as it gets, but a whimsical flowing top edge gives it just enough of a fun look to make it stand out. All it took was a little creative jigsaw work and a bit of extra time. It's a small investment for what turned out to be a very nice presentation.

MAKE YOUR FENCE FOLLOW YOUR SLOPE. Tall fences create the visual impression of a more expansive space. They also create a flow, as can be seen in this complex landscape design. The direction of the boards in the fence leads the eye back through the landscape, from the entrance to the thick vegetation in the garden area. The fence is also used to hang potted plants, giving it an additional decorative purpose. With modest finials, this is a very handsome structure that serves the landscape well.

Natural Borders

SHRUB ROWS MAKE AN ORDERLY BORDER. The beauty of using a row of trimmed shrubs as a landscape boundary is that it creates a soft and indistinct border that doesn't present an abrupt wall. You can create a lush living boundary like this quite easily even inside a fence. The use of tall repetitive shapes in this border reinforces the semi-formal style of the landscape.

EVERGREENS PROVIDE YEAR-ROUND PRIVACY. Pool privacy is often a key concern in landscaping a yard around one of these luxury features. Here, that challenge has been answered with a stand of evergreen trees, massed with a variety of sturdy shrubs. It creates an impenetrable privacy screen and an intriguing variable surface that seems to fade into darkness behind. This is an excellent way to cloak a manmade feature in natural surroundings that improve the look of both.

CAREFUL PRUNING CAN BECOME AN OBSESSION. Formal landscapes are perfectly accented with shaped shrub barriers and borders. The large lawn here is separated from a formal garden by a stately wall of shrubs that have been carefully cultivated and pruned to become a single wall of green. Adding to the site is an impressive archway of trained shrub branches that frames the passage between lawn and garden. If you have the patience and willingness to spend many hours on painstakingly detailed pruning, you can re-create this look with your own evergreen shrubs—on a smaller or larger scale.

Landscaping for Purpose

The desire for a beautiful outdoor space is usually reason enough to create a well-thought-out landscape design. There are, however, many other reasons, including practical goals that you need the landscape design to address.

Many of these purposes are related to how you use your yard. One of the most common purposes behind a landscape design or redesign is to create an outdoor entertainment area. This might mean making the area around a pool not only more attractive, but also more amenable to sunbathing and nightime entertaining. Entertainment often includes meals—whether family meals or food for guests during parties. That's why many landscape designs include both a cooking area (which can range from a grill in the corner of the patio to a full-blown outdoor kitchen) and an eating area. Both of these should be given adequate, well-laid-out space, as well as a beautiful view to enjoy while preparing or cooking food.

Other purposes are imposed upon the landscape by realities of geographic location or local regulations. Chief among these is conserving precious water. Lush landscape plantings are generally thirsty things, as are lawns of any size. States in the southwest and west often need to restrict water use in the hottest months of the year, but water conservation is an issue in almost every state. Water-conserving xeriscapes are a stylish way to deal with that issue.

It doesn't matter what purpose inspires your particular landscape; if it's compelling, your landscape should be designed to respond to it. That doesn't mean a less-than-attractive landscape, it just may mean a different type of chic. Regardless of the purpose, keep in mind that style never need be sacrificed in the name of function.

A GOOD LANDSCAPE PLAN KNITS YARD ELEMENTS TOGETHER. An amazingly varied landscape deserves to have its complexity appreciated. This large yard features an inviting lawn, stands of flowering shrubs, and a dry arroyo, with a pool providing a recreation area. It's meant for viewing. A long thin deck serves as both a walkway access to the pool, and as a viewing platform from which to enjoy the vista. If you've gone to the trouble to put together a thoughtful landscape design, make sure every part of it is seen from one vantage point or another.

LET YOUR LANDSCAPE GO CRAZY WITH COLOR. Create a showcase view from a pathway by "mounding" plants one on top of another up a slope. This technique creates layers of colors, textures, and mass that are alluring and delightful. The designer of this garden slope centered the appearance on the large yellow figure of a euphorbia, with sprinklings of fuchsia tulips throughout, and a supporting cast of less flashy plants that still add shape and texture.

KEEP POINT-OF-VIEW IN MIND WHEN DESIGNING. As this scene shows, a panorama of dense growth is an endlessly fascinating view, but positioning seating to take advantage of a sunset only enhances the landscaping and hardscaping.

TAKE A 360° APPROACH. A wild garden like this is all about multiple viewing perspectives. As someone strolls through this thickly planted garden, every turn and every step brings a different perspective. The idea in creating the design—and one that works well with many landscape styles—is to present a wholly different scene depending on where you're standing and which way you're looking. Every vantage yields an unexpected visual, making any visit to this landscape unique.

LANDSCAPING IS LARGELY ABOUT STAGING. Any elevated surface in the landscape should be thought of as a potential viewing platform. Here, a raised patio has been thoughtfully surrounded with a mix of evergreen shapes and sizes and an interesting scattering of flowering plants. The best landscapes offer a panoramic display that gives something interesting to see no matter where one sits on the hardscape surface. It's a good rule of thumb to follow whenever you are designing a landscape around a patio or deck.

MOVE YOUR VISION TO THE HIGHLIGHTS YOU CHERISH. There are several ways to control the view and the viewer in your landscape. One of the simplest is to point viewers toward what you want them to see. As this gardenscape clearly shows, that's easily done with a straight path that terminates in the focal point. This is a formal device; you can achieve the same end in a more informal landscape by directing a path by a focal feature and then adding a half-circle hardscape cutout alongside the path, overlooking a water feature, distinctive planting, or sculpture. Always know what feature you want to highlight in your landscape.

BIRDS AND BUTTERFLIES LOVE BRIGHT COLORS. A mix of deciduous and evergreen trees, shrubs, and flowering plants ensures that a variety of birds, butterflies, and other wildlife will visit your landscape. Different species of birds will nest and congregate in different trees, so the greater variety you have in your landscape—such as the many different types in this large yard—the more spectacular your bird-watching will be. Depending on the species, flowering plants will attract lovely butterflies and the bees essential to pollination. Just be aware that you can't be selective. The more inviting your yard, the more types of wildlife will visit it, including local dogs and cats, raccoons, and flower-eating deer. Plan for a tall fence if you want to keep non-winged creatures out.

THE BEST COURTS BLEND IN. When designing a recreational area into a landscape, small details help integrate the area into the larger landscape scene. This bocce ball court is edged with the same concrete treatment used on the steps up the slope, and a boulder in the corner of the court ties it to the boulder edging used throughout the landscape. You can use similar style indicators whether you're adding a hot tub or a horseshoe pit.

BECOME A BACKYARD GREENSKEEPER. Just as a landscape offers the potential for incredible beauty, it also provides endless possibilities for outdoor recreation. Putting greens are a wonderful landscape feature for the golf enthusiast who wants to work on his short game in his free time. Advances in artificial turf make greens such as these easier to install and maintain, and much nicer looking, than they once were. But even when focusing on a recreational feature such as this, don't sacrifice sound design. Notice how the shape of this green has been thoughtfully blended into the surrounding landscape and designed around older trees and shrubs.

Conserving Water

CHOOSE EFFICIENT WATER FEATURES. If you're lucky enough to have a Mediterranean-style house, follow the architecture's lead in designing your landscaping. Stone tiled courtyards are elegant stylistic flourishes, and a decorative fountain is the perfect focal point. Hot-weather plants are added in containers to ensure their longevity. Restricting plants to containers is an excellent xeriscape technique that you can put to use in your yard.

PRACTICE XERISCAPING STRATEGIES. A typical xeriscaped yard, like the one fronting this modern house, features spiky plants with judicious spacing between them. This is actually more of a planned layout than it looks. Because each plant needs to make best use of available water, you need to give each one a relatively large area of soil in which it can draw moisture. When properly designed, the spacing between plants creates a rhythm that draws the eye through the landscape's composition.

CHOOSE LOW-CONSUMING PLANTS FOR ARID CLIMATES. Extremely hot climates make their own rules, because the plants that can survive in a hot, arid landscape are limited. That's not to say a desert landscape can't be full of interest; unlike many xeriscapes that are designed with horizontal plantings, this yard features tall, vertical plants, including a focal point saguaro cactus, towering scrub oaks, and hot-weather flowering shrubs. The homeowner has taken landscaping cues from the environment, with a crushed stone pathway and split-rail fence.

CONTROL WATER RUNOFF. Concrete walkways and patios are natural complements to a low-water landscapes. The appearance of a concrete surface naturally looks great next to a grouping of succulents; this border along a concrete path is a perfect example. There's also a practical reason for using concrete as xeriscape hard surfaces: any water from rain or sprinklers runs right off it, benefiting the nearby plants. Wood, porous stone, or loose infill paths will just soak up excess moisture.

CREATE AN ARROYO. An arroyo is a faux water feature. As shown here, it is a reproduction of dry creek bed. The arroyo can actually serve a useful function in wet areas of the country, drawing water from a downspout away from the house to a dry well or other drain. In drier locales, the arroyo provides much of the visual fascination—in its shape and rock-strewn bed—that a stream or pond would in any other landscape. They are often used in desert landscapes, but as design elements, they are well suited to just about any landscape.

RESEARCH TO FIND EYE-POPPING DROUGHT-TOLERANT PLANTS. Designing a xeriscape does not mean that you have to automatically turn to cacti and succulents. As this backyard shows, a dry-climate yard can feature rich color and full-bodied shapes. The trick is to carefully select drought-tolerant flowering shrubs, trees, and ornamental grasses. There are plenty of options, so conserving water should never be an excuse for boring plantings with little variety.

USE NONLIVING ELEMENTS TO INTRODUCE COLOR. A water-conserving landscape design often focuses on colorful sculptural elements such as the green glazed urn in this backyard. The plants are chosen for their ability to thrive in heat and with little moisture, but a great amount of visual interest has been added by using several different types of rocks and stone. The red boulder actually complements the color of the urn, and the urn sits on a surface of river rocks. The path is actually finely crushed stone, and the whole look says "desert" without saying "dead."

Lighting the Landscape

Lighting is sometimes the forgotten landscape element. It's easy to disregard because in reality, most landscape designs see far more use during the day. But if you've gone to the effort and expense to design and create a truly thoughtful, interesting and attractive landscape, why not ensure that it can be used and enjoyed at any time?

Aside from making the space more usable after the sun goes down, landscape lighting holds great potential as a design feature itself. The right lighting in the right place will create a mood and emphasize your favorite parts of the design. And that's not even counting how beautiful the fixtures themselves can be. Lighting fixtures come in a mind-boggling variety of design styles, from subtle to magnificent.

Of course, function has to accompany form when it comes to lighting. Always start your landscaping plan with the illumination you need for safety—for getting in and out of pools and hot tubs and navigating pathways in the dark. You'll also pick from several different types of lights. If you only need modest pathway lighting for any area that receives significant sun exposure during the day, solar powered fixtures might work for your purposes. Where you're looking for a more complex lighting arrangement, you can use low-voltage systems that will save energy and provide slightly less light, or full-voltage wired-in fixtures.

Whatever type of lighting you settle on, always preview the landscape at night when you make your plan—that's when the lighting needs will be most obvious.

LIGHT THE POOL FIRST. A large, multi-featured landscape calls for diverse and layered approach to lighting. The lighting around this densely planted pool area starts with the lights in the pool itself, which are low-key and fairly dim. Strategically placed lighting in the rock surround ensures safety in getting in and out of the pool, as does the standard path lighting that has been discretely positioned along the walkway. Highlights throughout the canopy of the trees and large plants create drama and are more for mood than function. If your yard is large or your landscape is varied, use more than one type of lighting for best effect.

CHOOSE LIGHTING WITH RHYTHM AND BALANCE. Simply lighting every planting equally creates a bland nighttime scene. As this stately landscape shows, the better technique is to pick and choose a selection of plants to be lit and light them according to form: uplights for vertical trees, shrubs, and grasses; downlights for rock formations and low-growing flowering plants; and broadcast lights for pathways and other general areas.

UPLIGHT FOR INTEREST. Uplighting is most popular for landscapes because it creates a sense of drama. The trick is to position the lights where they will wash over the most foliage rather than shooting off into the sky. The lights need to be strong or the effect won't work. The denser the canopy of growth, the better. In this particular landscape, the variety of foliage and branch types creates even more intense visual interest than there would be in uplighting a copse of the same species of tree.

CHOOSE SOLAR PATHWAY LIGHTS FOR EASE OF INSTALLATION. Often, the post of the light is formed to a point so that the fixture can simply be stuck into the ground along a path.

USE LANDSCAPE LIGHTS AS DESIGN ACCENTS. A traditional and very attractive style of landscape lighting fixture is called the "hook and lantern," similar to what criers carried long ago through town squares. But even with a fetching style such as this, there are two ways to go with the fixtures. The more sedate design (left) blends in when when unlit, colored to match the mulch and soil. It's still a good-looking fixture, but illumination is the main goal. You can also make this style pop with craftsman-style interior fixtures (above), which add a bit of flair to the light they emit. Both styles are wired-in fixtures, meant to last a long time.

LOW-VOLTAGE LANDSCAPE LIGHTS OFFER MORE LIGHT OPTIONS THAN SOLAR-POWERED. Low-voltage halogen fixtures are some of the most popular for the ease of installation and bright attractive light. Many outdoor halogen fixtures offer some level of flexibility so that you can change the lighting as the landscape changes. Other fixtures are meant to direct the light in a purposeful way. Here, the fixture is simply intended to highlight a rock composition in the garden, supplementing stronger lighting on the patio.

UNDERSTANDING LOW-VOLTAGE COMPONENTS ▶

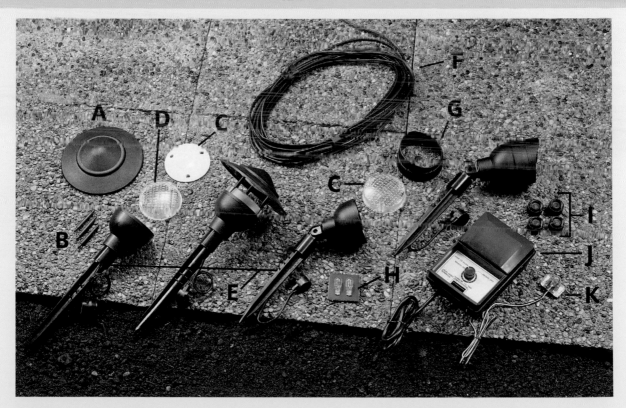

The parts of a low-voltage system are fairly basic and easy to work with. A typical system includes: lens cap (A); lens cap posts (B); upper reflector (C); lens (D); base/stake/cable connector assembly (contains lower reflector) (E); low-voltage cable (F); lens hood (G); 7-watt 12-volt bulbs (H); cable connector caps (I); control box containing transformer and timer (J); and light sensor (K).

Light Fixtures

THINK ABOUT DAYTIME APPEARANCE. The best landscape lighting fixtures provide as much visual interest during the day as they do during the night—just in a different way. As these interesting copper-plated fixtures show, fixtures can stand out as decorative elements themselves. Copper is a natural look and finish to add into a landscape, partly because the surface will develop a fetching green patina over time and exposure to the elements, unless sealed against it. These fixtures, however, will be bright and shiny for a long time to come; it's a great look and the fixture shapes only add to the effect.

GET A LITTLE FANCY WITH FORM. Lighting manufacturers have gone to great extents to create incredible fixture designs specifically for gardens and finely designed landscapes. In contrast to earlier plain, utilitarian pathway lights, fixture design such as this brings almost as much visual impact as a living addition would in a garden bed. This fixture includes two smaller "offshoots," creating a delightfully unexpected illuminated floral to the landscape.

INCLUDE CANDLES AND FLAMES IN YOUR LIGHTING PLAN. Look beyond wired-in lighting for maximum flexibility in your outdoor room illumination. Although installed pathway and hardscape lighting often accounts for the strongest light sources, consider combinations for your outdoor lighting plan. The intimate patio here includes ambient lighting from inside the house, the direct beam from a safety light on the side of the house, candles in hurricane lamps, and the homey glow from a chiminea.

CAPTURE REFLECTIONS. Uplights are often the best nighttime accent for swimming pools, because most pools already have lights under the water. A wonderful result of directing light away from the surface of the water on nearby objects or vegetation is that the water often reflects images from the landscaping. It's an alluring benefit, one that you should experiment with in positioning lights to their best advantage.

Photo Credits

Page 4, Photo courtesy of Borst Landscape and Design, photo by Kathy King, borstlandscape.com, 201-485-7779

Page 5 top, Photo courtesy of Luciole Design, Inc., www.lucioledesign.com, (916) 972-1809

Page 6 top, Shutterstock

Page 6 bottom right, iStock © Dan Brandenburg

Page 7, Photo courtesy of Luciole Design, Inc., www.lucioledesign.com, (916) 972-1809

Page 8, Shutterstock

Page 9 bottom, iStock

Page 10 both, Photo courtesy of Luciole Design, Inc., www.lucioledesign.com, (916) 972-1809

Page 11 both, Photo courtesy of Flowers' Gardens & Landscapes www.f10wersgardenslandscapes.com, (972) 429-7707

Page 12, Belgard/www.belgard.biz

Page 13 top, Photo courtesy of Luciole Design, Inc., www.lucioledesign.com, (916) 972-1809

Page 13 bottom, Shutterstock

Page 14 top, Shelley Metcalf

Page 14 bottom, Saxon Holt

Page 15 both, Shutterstock

Page 16 top, Photo courtesy of Architectural Landscape Design, Inc., billripley.com, 888.209.7206

Page 17 both, Photo courtesy of Architectural Landscape Design, Inc., billripley.com, 888.209.7206

Page 18 both, Shutterstock

Page 19 top, Shutterstock

Page 19 bottom, Saxon Holt Photography/photobotanic.com

Page 20 top, Photo courtesy of Architectural Landscape Design, Inc., billripley.com, 888.209.7206

Page 20 bottom, Shutterstock

Page 21 top, Shutterstock

Page 21 bottom, Photolibrary (CorbisInsideOutPix)

Page 22 top, Karen Melvin

Page 22 bottom, iStock

Page 23 top, Shutterstock

Page 23 bottom, Photo courtesy of Parker Homescape, parkerhomescape.com, (908) 626-1100

Page 24 both, Shutterstock

Page 25 both, Shutterstock

Page 26 top, John Gregor/ColdSnap Photography

Page 26 bottom, Garden Picture Library/Photolibrary.com ©Jean-Claude Hurni/Garden Picture Library

Page 27 top, iStock

Page 27 bottom, Jerry Pavia/Jerry Pavia Photography, Inc.

Page 28, Photo courtesy of Astrid Gaiser Garden Design, LLC, www.astridgaiser.com, (650) 224-2895

Page 29 top, Jessie Walker

Page 29 bottom, Brian Vanden Brink

Page 30 top left, Photo courtesy of Astrid Gaiser Garden Design, LLC, www.astridgaiser.com, (650) 224-2895

Page 30 top right, Photo courtesy of Pam August Landscape Design, www.pamaugust.com, (713) 858.6882

Page 30 bottom left and right, Photos courtesy of Architectural Landscape Design, Inc., billripley.com. 888.209.7206

Page 31 bottom, Photo courtesy of Astrid Gaiser Garden Design, LLC, www.astridgaiser.com, (650) 224-2895

Page 33 top, Shutterstock

Page 33 bottom, Photo courtesy of Borst Landscape and Design, photo by Kathy King, borstlandscape.com, 201-485-7779

Page 34 top, Photo courtesy of Borst Landscape and Design, photo by Kathy King, borstlandscape.com, 201-485-7779

Page 34 bottom, Photo courtesy of Flowers' Gardens & Landscapes www.f10wersgardenslandscapes.com, (972) 429-7707

Page 35 top left and right, Photo courtesy of Parker Homescape, parkerhomescape.com, (908) 626-1100

Page 35 bottom, Shutterstock

Page 36 both, Photo courtesy of Christensen Landscape www.christensenlandscape.com, (203) 484-0424

Page 37 top, Photo courtesy of Architectural Landscape Design, Inc., billripley.com, 888.209.7206

Page 37 bottom, Shutterstock

Page 38 both, Shutterstock

Page 39 both, Shutterstock

Page 40, Photo courtesy of Rosmarin Landscape Design annrosmarin.com, (216) 932-4859

Page 41, Photo courtesy of Borst Landscape and Design, photo by Kathy King, borstlandscape.com, 201-485-7779

Page 42 both, Photo courtesy of Borst Landscape and Design, photo by Kathy King, borstlandscape.com, 201-485-7779

Page 43 top, Photo courtesy of Maria von Brincken Landscape Garden Design, www.mariavonbrincken.com, (978) 443-4540

Page 43 bottom, Photo courtesy of Joyce K. Williams Landscape Design, www.chathamlandscapedesign.com, (508) 304-2996

Page 44 bottom, Shutterstock

Page 45 top, Shutterstock

Page 45 bottom, Photo courtesy of Rosmarin Landscape Design annrosmarin.com, (216) 932-4859

Page 46 both, Photo courtesy of Flowers' Gardens & Landscapes www.f10wersgardenslandscapes.com, (972) 429-7707

Page 47 both, Shutterstock

Page 48 both, Photo courtesy of Flowers' Gardens & Landscapes www.f10wersgardenslandscapes.com, (972) 429-7707

Page 49 both, Photo courtesy of Pam August Landscape Design, www.pamaugust.com, (713) 858.6882

Page 50 top, Photo courtesy of Flowers' Gardens & Landscapes www.f10wersgardenslandscapes.com, (972) 429-7707

Page 50 bottom, Charles Mann

Page 51 top, Jerry Pavia

Page 51 bottom, Photo courtesy of Rosmarin Landscape Design annrosmarin.com, (216) 932-4859

Page 52, Photo courtesy of Borst Landscape and Design, photo by John Baumgartner, borstlandscape.com, 201-485-7779

Page 53 left, Versa-LOK® Retaining Wall Systems/www.versa-lok.com

Page 53 right, Jerry Pavia

Page 56, Photo courtesy of Borst Landscape and Design, borstlandscape.com, 201-485-7779

Page 57 top, Photo courtesy of Barbara Lycett Landscape Design, blycettlandscapes.com, (206) 784-2521

Page 57 bottom left and right, Photo courtesy of Judy Nauseef Landscape Design, www.judynauseeflandscapedesign.com, (319) 337-7032

Page 58 top, Photo courtesy of Maria von Brincken Landscape Garden Design, www.mariavonbrincken.com, (978) 443-4540

Page 58 bottom, Photo courtesy of Parker Homescape, parkerhomescape.com, (908) 626-1100

Page 59 top, Shutterstock

Page 59 bottom, Shelley Metcalf

Page 60 top, Shelley Metcalf

Page 60 bottom, Photo courtesy of Albright-Souza Garden Design, www.albrightsouza.com, (83 l) 419-5994

Page 61 left, Shutterstock

Page 61 right, Jerry Pavia

Page 62 top, Shutterstock

Page 62 bottom, Jerry Pavia

Page 63, iStock

Page 64, Jerry Pavia

Page 65 both, Shutterstock

Page 66 both, Shutterstock

Page 67, Shutterstock

Page 68 top, Photo courtesy of Joyce K. Williams Landscape Design, www.chathamlandscapedesign.com, (508) 304-2996

Page 68 bottom, Shutterstock

Page 69 left, Shutterstock

Page 69 right, Jerry Pavia

Page 70 top, Photolibrary/Garden Picture Library/ www.photolibrary.com © Ron Sutherland

Page 70 bottom, Creative Publishing international

Page 71 top, Shelley Metcalf

Page 71 bottom, Photo courtesy of River City Landscaping, Inc., www.rivercitylandscaping.com. (916) 729-3586. Photo by Beth Abalos

Page 72 left, Photo courtesy of River City Landscaping, Inc., www.rivercitylandscaping.com. (916) 729-3586. Photo by Beth Abalos

Page 72 right and bottom, Photo courtesy of Prassas Landscape Studio, LLC, prassaslandscapestudio.com, (773) 879-9048

Page 73 top, Belgard

Page 73 bottom, Photo courtesy of Rosmarin Landscape Design annrosmarin.com, (216) 932-4859

Page 74 both, Shutterstock

Page 75, Shutterstock

Page 76, Shutterstock

Page 77 left, Photo courtesy of Prassas Landscape Studio, LLC, prassaslandscapestudio.com, (773) 879-9048

Page 77 right, Shutterstock

Page 78, Shutterstock

Page 79 top, Photo courtesy of Pacific Outdoor Living, www.pacificoutdoorliving.com, (888) 600-7224

Page 79 bottom, Shutterstock

Page 80, Shutterstock

Page 81, Shutterstock

Page 82 top, Photo courtesy of Pam August Landscape Design, www.pamaugust.com, (713) 858.6882

Page 82 bottom, Shutterstock

Page 83 top, Photo courtesy of Pacific Outdoor Living, www.pacificoutdoorliving.com, (888) 600-7224

Page 83 bottom, Shutterstock

Page 84 top, Photo courtesy of Christensen Landscape www.christensenlandscape.com, (203) 484-0424

Page 84 bottom, Shutterstock

Page 85, Photo courtesy of Joyce K. Williams Landscape Design, www.chathamlandscapedesign.com, (508) 304-2996

Page 86 top, Shelley Metcalf

Page 86 bottom, Photo courtesy of Rosmarin Landscape Design annrosmarin.com, (216) 932-4859

Page 87, Shutterstock

Page 88 top, Photo courtesy of Charleston Gardens, www.charlestongardens.com, (800) 469-0118

Page 88 bottom, Shutterstock

Page 89, Shelley Metcalf

Page 90 top, Creative Publishing international

Page 90 bottom, Photo courtesy of Pacific Outdoor Living, www.pacificoutdoorliving.com, (888) 600-7224

Page 91 top, Clive Nichols; Designer: Jane Mooney (bright blue wall and raised bed planted with herbaceous plants); Sculpture by John Brown

Page 91 bottom, Jerry Pavia

Page 92 top, Creative Publishing international

Page 92 bottom, Shutterstock

Page 93, Shutterstock

Page 94 top, Photo courtesy of Maria von Brincken Landscape Garden Design, www.mariavonbrincken.com, (978) 443-4540

Page 94 bottom left, Photo courtesy of Joyce K. Williams Landscape Design, www.chathamlandscapedesign.com, (508) 304-2996

Page 94 bottom right, Photo courtesy of Judy Nauseef Landscape Design, www.judynauseeflandscapedesign.com, (319) 337-7032

Page 95 all, Photo courtesy of Joyce K. Williams Landscape Design, www.chathamlandscapedesign.com, (508) 304-2996

Page 96 top, Photo courtesy of Maria von Brincken Landscape Garden Design, www.mariavonbrincken.com, (978) 443-4540

Page 96 bottom, Photo courtesy of Joyce K. Williams Landscape Design, www.chathamlandscapedesign.com, (508) 304-2996

Page 97 top, Jerry Pavia

Page 97 bottom, Shutterstock

Page 98 top, Photo courtesy of Barbara Lycett Landscape Design, blycettlandscapes.com, (200) 784-2521

Page 98 bottom, Shutterstock

Page 99 top, Photo courtesy of Borst Landscape and Design, borstlandscape.com, 201-485-7779

Page 99 bottom, Photo courtesy of Pacific Outdoor Living, www.pacificoutdoorliving.com, (888) 600-7224

Page 100 both, Shutterstock

Page 101 both, Shutterstock

Page 102 both, Shutterstock

Page 103, Shutterstock

Page 104 top, Photo courtesy of Pacific Outdoor Living, www.pacificoutdoorliving.com, (888) 600-7224

Page 104 bottom, Photo courtesy of Christensen Landscape www.christensenlandscape.com, (203) 484-0424

Page 105, Shutterstock

Page 106, Shutterstock

Page 107 top, Shutterstock

Page 107 bottom, Photo courtesy of Pacific Outdoor Living, www.pacificoutdoorliving.com, (888) 600-7224

Page 108, Creative Publishing international

Page 109 both, Photo courtesy of Borst Landscape and Design, photo by John Baumgartner, borstlandscape.com, 201-485-7779

Page 110 top, Photo courtesy of Rosmarin Landscape Design annrosmarin.com, (216) 932-4859

Page 110 bottom, Shutterstock

Page 111 both, Shutterstock

Page 112 top, Photo courtesy of Rosmarin Landscape Design annrosmarin.com, (216) 932-4859

Page 112 bottom, Photo courtesy of Joyce K. Williams Landscape Design, www.chathamlandscapedesign.com, (508) 304-2996

Page 113, Shutterstock

Page 114 top, Photo courtesy of Flowers' Gardens & Landscapes www.f1owersgardenslandscapes.com, (972) 429-7707

Page 114 bottom, Photo courtesy of Borst Landscape and Design, photo by Kathy King, borstlandscape.com, 201-485-7779

Page 115 top, Photo courtesy of Maria von Brincken Landscape Garden Design, www.mariavonbrincken.com, (978) 443-4540

Page 115 bottom, Shutterstock

Page 116 top left, Photo courtesy of River City Landscaping, Inc., www.rivercitylandscaping.com. (916) 729-3586. Photo by Rick Abalos

Page 116 top right, Photo courtesy of Charleston Gardens, www.charlestongardens.com, (800) 469-0118

Page 116 bottom, Shutterstock

Page 117, Jerry Pavia

Page 118 top left and right, Photo courtesy of Flowers' Gardens & Landscapes www.f1owersgardenslandscapes.com, (972) 429-7707

Page 118 bottom, Photo courtesy of Borst Landscape and Design, photo by John Baumgartner, borstlandscape.com, 201-485-7779

Page 119 top, Shutterstock

Page 119 bottom, Photo courtesy of Luciole Design, Inc., www.lucioledesign.com, (916) 972-1809

Page 120 both, Shutterstock

Page 121 top, Photo courtesy of Joyce K. Williams Landscape Design, www.chathamlandscapedesign.com, (508) 304-2996

Page 121 bottom, Shutterstock

Page 122 top, Shutterstock

Page 122 bottom left, Shutterstock

Page 122 bottom right, Photo courtesy of Charleston Gardens, www.charlestongardens.com, (800) 469-0118

Page 123 top, Shutterstock

Page 123 bottom, Photo courtesy of Pam August Landscape Design, www.pamaugust.com, (713) 858.6882

Page 124 top, Photo courtesy of Flowers' Gardens & Landscapes www.f1owersgardenslandscapes.com, (972) 429-7707

Page 124 bottom, Photo courtesy of Pam August Landscape Design, www.pamaugust.com, (713) 858.6882

Page 125 top, Photo courtesy of River City Landscaping, Inc., www.rivercitylandscaping.com. (916) 729-3586. Photo by Rick Abalos

Page 125 bottom, Photo courtesy of Charleston Gardens, www.charlestongardens.com, (800) 469-0118

Page 126 top, Shutterstock

Page 126 bottom, Photo courtesy of Luciole Design, Inc., www.lucioledesign.com, (916) 972-1809

Page 127 top left, Shutterstock

Page 127 top right, Photo courtesy of Joyce K. Williams Landscape Design, www.chathamlandscapedesign.com, (508) 304-2996

Page 127 bottom, Photo courtesy of Albright-Souza Garden Design, www.albrightsouza.com, (83 l) 419-5994

Page 128 top, Photo courtesy of Pam August Landscape Design, www.pamaugust.com, (713) 858.6882

Page 128 bottom, Photo courtesy of Charleston Gardens, www.charlestongardens.com, (800) 469-0118

Page 129, Shutterstock

Page 130, Photo courtesy of Borst Landscape and Design, photo by Kathy King, borstlandscape.com, 201-485-7779

Page 131 top, Shutterstock

Page 131 bottom, Photo courtesy of Joyce K. Williams Landscape Design, www.chathamlandscapedesign.com, (508) 304-2996

Page 132 top left, Shutterstock

Page 132 top right and bottom, Brian Vanden Brink

Page 133, Walpole Workers

Page 134 top, John Gregor/ColdSnap Photography ©John Gregor/ColdSnap Photography

Page 134 bottom, Photo courtesy of Rosmarin Landscape Design annrosmarin.com, (216) 932 4859

Page 135 top, Walpole Woodworkers

Page 135 bottom, California Redwood Association, www.calredwood.com, 888-CALREDWOOD by Charles Callister, Jr. for Julian Hedges

Page 136 top, Jerry Pavia

Page 136 bottom, Walpole Woodworkers

Page 137 top left, Walpole Woodworkers

Page 137 top right and bottom, Creative Publishing international

Page 138 both, Jerry Pavia

Page 139, Charles Mann

Page 140 top, Photolibrary/Garden Picture Library/www.photolibrary.com © Ed Badham

Page 140 bottom, Photo courtesy of Parker Homescape, parkerhomescape.com, (908) 626-1100

Page 141 top, Shutterstock

Page 141 bottom, Photolibrary/Garden Picture Library/www.photolibrary.com © Jennifer Cheung/Botanica/GPL

Page 142 top left and right, Shutterstock

Page 142 bottom, Photo courtesy of Albright-Souza Garden Design, www.albrightsouza.com, (83 l) 419-5994

Page 143 top, Shutterstock

Page 143 bottom, Creative Publishing international

Page 144 top, Photo courtesy of Charleston Gardens, www.charlestongardens.com, (800) 469-0118

Page 144 bottom, Jerry Pavia

Page 145 top left and right, Photo courtesy of Astrid Gaiser Garden Design, LLC, www.astridgaiser.com, (650) 224-2895

Page 145 bottom, Photo courtesy of Joyce K. Williams Landscape Design, www.chathamlandscapedesign.com, (508) 304-2996

Page 146 both, Shutterstock

Photo Credits

Page 147 both, Shutterstock
Page 148, California Redwoos Association
Page 149 top left and right, Photo courtesy of Christensen Landscape www.christensenlandscape.com, (203) 484-0424
Page 149 bottom, Shelley Metcalf/shelley.metcalf@cox.net
Page 150 top, Photo courtesy of Joyce K. Williams Landscape Design, www.chathamlandscapedesign.com, (508) 304-2996
Page 150 bottom, Photo courtesy of Flowers' Gardens & Landscapes www.f1owersgardenslandscapes.com, (972) 429-7707
Page 151 top, Photo courtesy of Flowers' Gardens & Landscapes www.f1owersgardenslandscapes.com, (972) 429-7707
Page 151 bottom, Tony Giammarino
Page 152 top, Creative Publishing international
Page 152 bottom, Photo courtesy of Luciole Design, Inc., www.lucioledesign.com, (916) 972-1809
Page 153 left, Tony Giammarino
Page 153 right, Photo courtesy of Flowers' Gardens & Landscapes www.f1owersgardenslandscapes.com, (972) 429-7707
Page 154 top and lower left, Photo courtesy of Flowers' Gardens & Landscapes www.f1owersgardenslandscapes.com, (972) 429-7707
Page 154 lower right, iStock
Page 155, Shutterstock
Page 156 top, Photo courtesy of Borst Landscape and Design, photo by Kathy King, borstlandscape.com, 201-485-7779
Page 156 bottom, Photo courtesy of Christensen Landscape www.christensenlandscape.com, (203) 484-0424
Page 157, Shutterstock
Page 158, Photo courtesy of Clemens Jellema, Fine Decks, Inc., www.finedecks.com
Page 159 top, Shutterstock
Page 159 bottom, Shelley Metcalf
Page 160 top, Shutterstock

Page 160 bottom, Photo courtesy of Joyce K. Williams Landscape Design, www.chathamlandscapedesign.com, (508) 304-2996
Page 161, Shutterstock
Page 162, Shutterstock
Page 163 top, Photo courtesy of Albright-Souza Garden Design, www.albrightsouza.com, (83 l) 419-5994
Page 163 bottom, Prosport
Page 164 both, Shutterstock
Page 165 top, Shutterstock
Page 165 bottom, Photolibrary/www.photolibrary.com
Page 166, Creative Publishing international
Page 167 both, Photo courtesy of Flowers' Gardens & Landscapes www.f1owersgardenslandscapes.com, (972) 429-7707
Page 168, Photo courtesy of Natural Concepts, www.natural-concepts.net, (281) 970-7800
Page 169 top, Shutterstock
Page 169 bottom, Photo courtesy of Natural Concepts, www.natural-concepts.net, (281) 970-7800
Page 170 top left, iStock
Page 170 right, Photo courtesy of Charleston Gardens, www.charlestongardens.com, (800) 469-0118
Page 171 top, Photo courtesy of Natural Concepts, www.natural-concepts.net, (281) 970-7800
Page 171 bottom, Creative Publishing international
Page 172 top, Photo courtesy of Astrid Gaiser Garden Design, LLC, www.astridgaiser.com, (650) 224-2895
Page 172 bottom, Photo courtesy of Charleston Gardens, www.charlestongardens.com, (800) 469-0118
Page 173 top, Shutterstock
Page 173 bottom, Photo courtesy of Borst Landscape and Design, photo by John Baumgartner, borstlandscape.com, 201-485-7779
Page 174, Photo courtesy of Natural Concepts, www.natural-concepts.net, (281) 970-7800

Resources

American Horticultural Society
You'll find information about plants, gardens, and more at this site.
www.ahs.org
(800) 777-7931

American Society of Landscape Architects (ASLA)
If you want to completely reimagine a large yard, you may want to turn to a landscape architect. Find one at the ASLA website, along with other information.
www.asla.org
(888) 999-ASLA

Association of Professional Landscape Designers (APLD)
Whether you just need a little assistance setting up a backyard garden or want to completely redo a large yard, you can member professionals in your area by perusing the listings on the APLD's website.
www.apld.com
(717) 238-9780

Black & Decker
Turn to B&D for all the tools you'll need to create and maintain your dream landscape.
www.blackanddecker.com

Charleston Gardens
A full-service retailer, Charleston Gardens offers just about anything you might want to include in your outdoor room, from sculptures, larger structures, birdbaths, and outdoor furnishings.
www.charlestongardens.com
(866) 469-0118

Frontgate
From simple and basic chaise lounges to incredibly sophisticated outdoor dining and living room sets, Frontgate furnishes landscapes regardless of style.
www.frontgate.com
(888) 263-9850

National Gardening Association
General information and resources related to gardening.
www.garden.org
(802) 863-5251